HIGH PERFORMANCE CORVETTES 1983-1989

Compiled by
R.M. Clarke

ISBN 1 870642 856

Distributed by
Brooklands Book Distribution Ltd.
'Holmerise', Seven Hills Road,
Cobham, Surrey, England
Printed in Hong Kong

BROOKLANDS BOOKS SERIES
AC Ace & Aceca 1953-1983
AC Cobra 1962-1969
Alfa Romeo Alfasud 1972-1984
Alfa Romeo Alfetta Coupes GT.GTV.GTV6 1974-1987
Alfa Romeo Giulia Berlinas 1962-1976
Alfa Romeo Giulia Coupés 1963-1976
Alfa Romeo Spider 1966-1987
Allard Gold Portfolio 1937-1958
Alvis Gold Portfolio 1919-1967
Aston Martin Gold Portfolio 1972-1985
Austin Seven 1922-1982
Austin A30 & A35 1951-1962
Austin Healey 3000 1959-1967
Austin Healey 100 & 3000 Collection No. 1
Austin Healey 'Frogeye' Sprite Collection No. 1
Austin Healey Sprite 1958-1971
Avanti 1962-1983
BMW Six Cylinder Coupés 1969-1975
BMW 1600 Collection No. 1
BMW 2002 1968-1976
Bristol Cars Gold Portfolio 1946-1985
Buick Automobiles 1947-1960
Buick Riviera 1963-1978
Cadillac Automobiles 1949-1959
Cadillac Automobiles 1960-1969
Cadillac Eldorado 1967-1978
Camaro 1966-1970
Chevrolet Camaro & Z-28 1973-1981
High Performance Camaros 1982-1988
Chevrolet Camaro Collection No. 1
Chevrolet 1955-1957
Chevrolet Impala & SS 1958-1971
Chevelle & SS 1964-1972
Chevy II Nova & SS 1962-1973
High Performance Corvettes 1983-1989
Chrysler 300 1955-1970
Citroen Traction Avant 1934-1957
Citroen DS & ID 1955-1975
Citroen 2CV 1948-1988
Cobras & Replicas 1962-1983
Cortina 1600E & GT 1967-1970
Corvair 1959-1968
Daimler Dart & V-8 250 1959-1969
Datsun 240Z 1970-1973
Datsun 280Z & ZX 1975-1983
De Tomaso Collection No. 1
Dodge Charger 1966-1974
Excalibur Collection No. 1
Ferrari Cars 1946-1956
Ferrari Dino 1965-1974
Ferrari Dino 308 1974-1979
Ferrari 308 & Mondial 1980-1984
Ferrari Collection No. 1
Fiat-Bertone X1/9 1973-1988
Fiat Pininfarina 124+2000 Spider 1968-1985
Ford Automobiles 1944-1959
Ford Fairlane 1955-1970
Ford Falcon 1960-1970
Ford RS Escort 1968-1980
Honda CRX 1983-1987
High Performance Escorts MkI 1968-1974
High Performance Escorts MkII 1975-1980
High Performance Mustangs 1982-1988
Hudson & Railton Cars 1936-1940
Jaguar Cars 1957-1961
Jaguar Cars 1961-1964
Jaguar XK120 XK140 XK150 Gold Portfolio 1948-1960
Jaguar MK2 1959-1969
Jaguar E-Type Gold Portfolio 1961-1971
Jaguar E-Type 1966-1971
Jaguar E-Type V12 1971-1975
Jaguar XJ6 1968-1972
Jaguar XJ6 Series II 1973-1979
Jaguar XJ6 & XJ12 Series III 1979-1985
Jaguar XJ12 1972-1980
Jaguar XJS Gold Portfolio 1975-1988
Jensen Cars 1946-1967
Jensen Cars 1967-1979
Jensen Interceptor Gold Portfolio 1966-1986
Jensen Healey 1972-1976
Lamborghini Cars 1964-1970
Lamborghini Cars 1970-1975
Lamborghini Countach Collection No. 1
Lamborghini Countach & Urraco 1974-1980
Lamborghini Countach & Jalpa 1980-1985
Lancia Stratos 1972-1985
Land Rover 1948-1973
Land Rover Series II & IIa 1958-1971
Land Rover Series III 1971-1985
Land Rover 90 & 110 1983-1989
Land Rover 90 & 110 1983-1989
Lotus Cortina 1963-1970
Lotur Elan Gold Portfolio 1962-1974
Lotus Elan Collection No. 2
Lotus Elite 1957-1964
Lotus Elite & Eclat 1974-1981
Lotus Turbo Esprit 1980-1986
Lotus Europa 1966-1975
Lotus Europa Collection No. 1
Lotus Seven 1957-1980
Lotus Seven Collection No. 1
Marcos Cars 1960-1988
Maserati 1965-1970
Maserati 1970-1975
Marcos Cars 1960-1988
Mazda RX-7 Collection No. 1
Mercedes 190 & 300SL 1954-1963
Mercedes 230/250/280SL 1963-1971
Mercedes 350/450SL & SLC 1971-1980
Mercedes Benz Cars 1949-1954
Mercedes Benz Cars 1954-1957
Mercedes Benz Cars 1957-1961
Mercedes Benz Competition Cars 1950-1957
Metropolitan 1954-1962
MG TC 1945-1949

MG TD 1949-1953
MG TF 1953-1955
MG Cars 1957-1959
MG Cars 1959-1962
MG Midget 1961-1980
MGA Collection No. 1
MGA Roadsters 1955-1962
MGB Roadsters 1962-1980
MGB GT 1965-1980
Mini Cooper 1961-1971
Morgan Cars 1960-1970
The Morgan 3-Weeler Gold Portfolio 1910-1952
Morgan Cars Gold Portfolio 1968-1989
Morris Minor Collection No. 1
Olosmobile Automobiles 1955-1963
Old's Cutlass & 4-4-2 1964-1972
Oldsmobile Toronado 1966-1978
Opel GT 1968-1973
Packard Gold Portfolio 1946-1958
Pantera 1970-1973
Pantera & Mangusta 1969-1974
Plymouth Barracuda 1964-1974
Pontiac Fiero 1984-1988
Pontiac Firebird 1967-1973
Pontiac Firebird and Trans-Am 1973-1981
High Performance Firebirds 1982-1988
Pontiac Tempest & GTO 1961-1965
Porsche Cars 1960-1964
Porsche Cars 1964-1968
Porsche Cars 1968-1972
Porsche Cars in the Sixties
Porsche Cars 1972-1975
Porsche 356 1952-1965
Porsche 911 1965-1969
Porsche 911 1970-1972
Porsche 911 1973-1977
Porsche 911 Carrera 1973-1977
Porsche 911 SC 1978-1983
Porsche 911 Turbo 1975-1984
Porsche 914 Gold Portfolio 1969-1976
Porsche 914 Collection No. 1
Porsche 924 Gold Portfolio 1975-1988
Porsche 928 1977-1989
Porsche 944 1981-1985
Reliant Scimitar 1964-1986
Riley 1½ & 2½ Litre Gold Portfolio 1945-1955
Rolls Royce Silver Cloud 1955-1965
Rolls Royce Silver Shadow 1965-1980
Range Rover Gold Portfolio 1970-1988
Rover 3 & 3.5 Litre 1958-1973
Rover P4 1949-1959
Rover P4 1955-1964
Rover 2000 + 2200 1963-1977
Rover 3500 1968-1977
Rover 3500 & Vitesse 1976-1986
Saab Sonett Collection No. 1
Saab Turbo 1976-1983
Studebaker Hawks & Larks 1956-1963
Sunbeam Tiger and Alpine Gold Portfolio 1959-1967
Thunderbird 1955-1957
Thunderbird 1958-1963
Thunderbird 1964-1976
Toyota MR2 1984-1988
Triumph 2000-2.5-2500 1963-1977
Triumph Spitfire 1962-1980
Triumph Spitfire Collection No. 1
Triumph Stag 1970-1980
Triumph Stag Collection No. 1
Triumph TR2 & TR3 1952-1960
Triumph TR4.TR5.TR250 1961-1968
Triumph TR6 1969-1976
Triumph TR6 Collection No. 1
Triumph TR7 & TR8 1975-1982
Triumph GT6 1966-1974
Triumph Vitesse & Herald 1959-1971
TVR Gold Portfolio 1959-1988
Volkswagen 1936-1956
VW Beetle 1956-1977
VW Beetle Collection No. 1
VW Golf GTi 1976-1986
VW Karmann Ghia 1955-1982
VW Scirocco 1974-1981
VW Bus-Camper-Van 1954-1967
VW Bus-Camper-Van 1968-1979
VW Bus-Camper-Van 1979-1989
Volvo 1800 1960-1973
Volvo 120 Series 1956-1970

BROOKLANDS MUSCLE CARS SERIES
American Motors Muscle Cars 1966-1970
Buick Muscle Cars 1965-1970
Camaro Muscle Cars 1966-1972
Capri Muscle Cars 1969-1983
Chevrolet Muscle Cars 1966-1972
Dodge Muscle Cars 1967-1970
Mercury Muscle Cars 1966-1971
Mini Muscle Cars 1961-1979
Mopar Muscle Cars 1964-1967
Mopar Muscle Cars 1968-1971
Mustang Muscle Cars 1967-1971
Shelby Mustang Muscle Cars 1965-1970
Oldsmobile Muscle Cars 1964-1970
Plymouth Muscle Cars 1965-1971
Pontiac Muscle Cars 1966-1972
Muscle Cars Compared Book 2 1965-1971

BROOKLANDS ROAD & TRACK SERIES
Road & Track on Alfa Romeo 1949-1963
Road & Track on Alfa Romeo 1964-1970
Road & Track on Alfa Romeo 1971-1976
Road & Track on Alfa Romeo 1977-1989
Road & Track on Aston Martin 1962-1984
Road & Track on Auburn Cord & Duesenberg 1952-1984
Road & Track on Audi 1952-1980
Road & Track on Audi 1980-1986
Road & Track on Austin Healey 1953-1970

Road & Track on BMW Cars 1966-1974
Road & Track on BMW Cars 1975-1978
Road & Track on BMW Cars 1979-1983
Road & Track on Cobra, Shelby &
Ford GT40 1962-1983
Road & Track on Corvette 1953-1967
Road & Track on Corvette 1968-1982
Road & Track on Corvette 1982-1986
Road & Track on Datsun Z 1970-1983
Road & Track on Ferrari 1950-1968
Road & Track on Ferrari 1968-1974
Road & Track on Ferrari 1975-1981
Road & Track on Ferrari 1981-1984
Road & Track on Fiat Sports Cars 1968-1987
Road & Track on Jaguar 1950-1960
Road & Track on Jaguar 1961-1968
Road & Track on Jaguar 1968-1974
Road & Track on Jaguar 1974-1982
Road & Track on Jaguar 1983-1989
Road & Track on Lamborghini 1964-1985
Road & Track on Lotus 1972-1981
Road & Track on Maserati 1952-1974
Road & Track on Maserati 1975-1983
Road & Track on Mazda RX7 1978-1986
Road & Track on Mercedes 1952-1962
Road & Track on Mercedes 1963-1970
Road & Track on Mercedes 1971-1979
Road & Track on Mercedes 1980-1987
Road & Track on MG Sports Cars 1949-1961
Road & Track on MG Sports Cars 1962-1980
Road & Track on Mustang 1964-1977
Road & Track on Peugeot 1955-1986
Road & Track on Pontiac 1960-1983
Road & Track on Porsche 1951-1967
Road & Track on Porsche 1968-1971
Road & Track on Porsche 1972-1975
Road & Track on Porsche 1975-1978
Road & Track on Porsche 1979-1982
Road & Track on Porsche 1982-1985
Road & Track on Porsche 1985-1988
Road & Track on Rolls Royce & Bentley 1950-1965
Road & Track on Rolls Royce & Bentley 1966-1984
Road & Track on Saab 1955-1985
Road & Track on Toyota Sports & G T Cars 1966-1986
Road & Track on Triumph Sports Cars 1953-1967
Road & Track on Triumph Sports Cars 1967-1974
Road & Track on Triumph Sports Cars 1974-1982
Road & Track on Volkswagen 1951-1968
Road & Track on Volkswagen 1968-1978
Road & Track on Volkswagen 1978-1985
Road & Track on Volvo 1957-1974
Road & Track on Volvo 1975-1985
Road & Track Henry Manney at Large & Abroad

BROOKLANDS CAR AND DRIVER SERIES
Car and Driver on BMW 1955-1977
Car and Driver on BMW 1977-1985
Car and Driver on Cobra, Shelby & Ford GT40
1963-1984
Car and Driver on Datsun Z 1600 & 2000
1966-1984
Car and Driver on Corvette 1956-1967
Car and Driver on Corvette 1968-1977
Car and Driver on Corvette 1978-1982
Car and Driver on Corvette 1983-1988
Car and Driver on Ferrari 1955-1962
Car and Driver on Ferrari 1963-1975
Car and Driver on Ferrari 1976-1983
Car and Driver on Mopar 1956-1967
Car and Driver on Mopar 1968-1975
Car and Driver on Mustang 1964-1972
Car and Driver on Pontiac 1961-1975
Car and Driver on Porsche 1955-1962
Car and Driver on Porsche 1963-1970
Car and Driver on Porsche 1970-1976
Car and Driver on Porsche 1977-1981
Car and Driver on Porsche 1982-1986
Car and Driver on Saab 1956-1985
Car and Driver on Volvo 1955-1986

BROOKLANDS MOTOR & THOROUGHBRED & CLASSIC CAR SERIES
Motor & T & CC on Ferrari 1966-1976
Motor & T & CC on Ferrari 1976-1984
Motor & T & CC on Lotus 1979-1983

BROOKLANDS PRACTICAL CLASSICS SERIES
Practical Classics on Austin A 40 Restoration
Practical Classics on Land Rover Restoration
Practical Classics on Metalworking in Restoration
Practical Classics on Midget/Sprite Restoration
Practical Classics on Mini Cooper Restoration
Practical Classics on MGB Restoration
Practical Classics on Morris Minor Restoration
Practical Classics on Triumph Herald/Vitesse
Practical Classics on Triumph Spitfire Restoration
Practical Classics on VW Beetle Restoration
Practical Classics on 1930S Car Restoration

BROOKLANDS MILITARY VEHICLES SERIES
Allied Military Vehicles Collection No. 1
Allied Military Vehicles Collection No. 2
Dodge Military Vehicles Collection No. 1
Military Jeeps 1941-1945
Off Road Jeeps 1944-1971
V W Kubelwagen 1940-1975

BROOKLANDS
BOOKS

CONTENTS

ACKNOWLEDGEMENTS

Brooklands Books have grown out of a hobby that started over thirty years ago, and have today become one of the most accessible works of reference for those that enjoy automobiles.

Some 11,000 stories can be located within their 350 titles. They cover in the main affordable post-war vehicles that can be bought, driven and cherished by ordinary people. Especially popular are books that report on the more powerful sporting cars, and last year we introduced three new titles covering recent Mustangs, Camaros and Firebirds. These have been in much demand and we were asked a few months ago if we could add Corvette to the list.

The latest Corvettes introduced in 1983 arrived with a tremendous fanfare and were well received by the motoring press when initially tested on the track. When driven under highway conditions however, their handling left a lot to be desired and much criticism was to follow. Chevrolet recognising the problem took prompt action and immediately went to work to improve the suspension of their sporting flagship. The outcome of their labours can be traced through the following stories.

The leading automotive publishers have for many years generously supported our series by allowing us to include their copyright road tests and other articles that make up these anthologies. I am sure that Corvette devotees will wish to join with us in thanking the management of Autocar, Automobile Magazine, Car South Africa, Car and Driver, Fast Lane, Hot Rod, Modern Motor, Motor Trend and Road & Track, for their understanding and ongoing help.

R.M. Clarke

CHEVROLET
CORVETTE

Give Corvette engineers some FRP and aluminum,
and they'll do something fabulous with it

PHOTOS BY JOHN LAMM

WHATEVER YOUR VIEWS of previous Corvettes—the ultimate street rumbler, America's only true sports car, outdated clunker, whatever—forget them. The new 5th-generation Corvette is here, bristling with fascinating technicalities and deserving a dedicated portion of any enthusiast's memory bank. Is it now the best exotic car in the world? The best exotic car value? Or merely an updated clunker?

To give us our first in-depth experience with the car, Chevrolet orchestrated a sequence of events that necessarily fell short of our usual road test procedure, yet was one helluva lot more informative than a few trips around GM Proving Ground's Black Lake. Reason for this was clear: the availability of only six Corvettes for a rather larger group of the world's automotive journalists. In fact, the six were in pilot car configuration; that is, cars built on the Bowling Green, Kentucky assembly line for evaluating components and procedures before actual production begins. Over a 2-week period, several staff members sampled the cars at various locations. These included a gale-swept Riverside International Raceway ("Forget the driving, folks, and adjourn to the tent. Forget the tent, folks."), the same raceway on a decidedly better day, Orange County International Raceway for our instrumented testing and Orange County Fairgrounds for our skidpad work. Also, our Engineering Editor took a 300-mile high-speed loop through the flatland and mountains inland from Santa Barbara, a pleasant trip that gave the new Corvette the kind of workout it loves best. What we didn't get to do for this report was ordinary day-to-day driving; some of those aspects are covered in the accompanying report on the 4+3 manual-transmission version, which was not introduced until several months into the new car's production life.

The new Corvette was our first 1984 test car, and it was barely

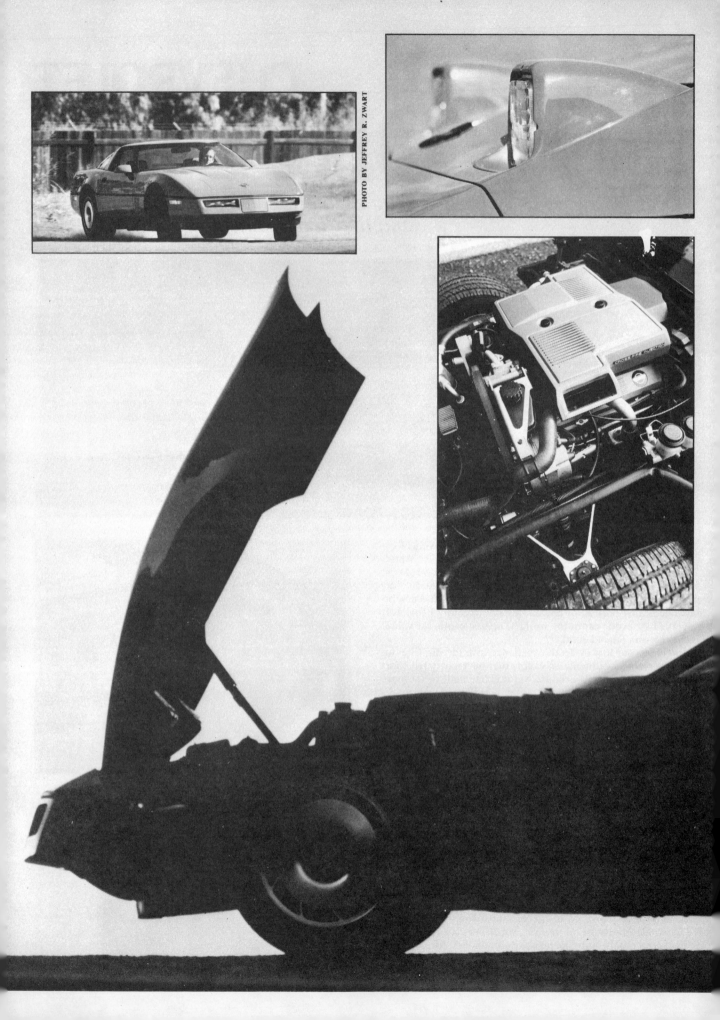

PHOTO BY JEFFREY R. ZWART

1983 when all this happened. That's because Chevrolet decided to leapfrog the 1983 model year and call the new car a 1984 Corvette.

Yes, a 1984, from spring 1983 on—what is happening to the sacred autumn season for new models here in America? Chevrolet isn't the only maker to do this either; the BMW 318i comes to mind as another example. In any case, for reasons lurking in EPA definitions of model year, corporate scheduling of startup and shift-over dates and, we suspect, some good ol'-fashioned hype, there were no 1983 Corvettes as such. Production began on January 3, 1983 and all Corvettes built between then and late summer 1984 will have vehicle identification numbers specifying 1984 as the model year.

This meant that the 1983 run of Corvettes had to meet 1984 emission standards, which are stricter in the sense that all the pollutant limits had to be met at all altitudes; previously, cars sold at high altitudes were tested differently.

This 1984-model business affects Corporate Average Fuel Economy and the Corvette's gas-guzzler tax status too. All Corvettes built between startup and the 1985 model year count toward the 1984 CAFE, up from 1983's 26.0 to 27.0 mpg in 1984. And for 1984 models the guzzler tax is triggered at 19.5 mpg, versus 19.0 in 1983. So the Chevrolet folk set themselves a harder task in these respects too when they decided to call their new car a 1984.

So much for regulations and strange model years. What of the car itself? Let's examine this new Corvette by starting at the road and working our way up, pausing along the way to share our road test results.

We focused on that Corvette with the enthusiast's suspension, the Z51 package. Its contact with the road comes with four Goodyear Eagle VR50s, P255/50VR-16s, mounted on mirror-matched finned alloy wheels, 16 x 8½ fronts and 16 x 9½ rears. As reported earlier in R&T ("Ampersand," January 1983), these Goodyears were developed especially for and in parallel with the new Corvette. If you're an enthusiast, your intellect is excited by their unidirectional tread pattern derived from Formula 1 rain rubber and your soul is enriched by their V rating (good for

sustained running above 130 mph). But if you're a Corvette engineer, their section width on the 9½ rear wheels also complicates your life. Seems that the rears stick out 4 mm beyond European regulations, so the export Corvette has to be fitted with 8½ wheels at the rear as well. Our non-Z51 (the base version, if you will) gets Goodyear Eagle GTs, P215/65R-15s, mounted on 15 x 7 and 15 x 7½ wheels, front and rear, respectively.

Whatever wheels, they mount to forged aluminum knuckles, front and rear. And these aren't the only nonferrous materials in the suspension. At the front, unequal-length A-arms are also elegant aluminum forgings. And gone are the previous coil springs, replaced by a transverse single-leaf spring of E-glass (the tough guy of the fiberglass clan) and epoxy. Though not interchangeable, it's akin to the FRP rear leaf introduced on the 1982 Corvette and carried over on this one. Among advantages of the front FRP leaf are 50 percent less weight, better packaging than coils and higher fatigue strength (a typical steel spring gets tired after 75,000 full compressions; one of FRP lasts beyond 5 million!). Tube shocks and an anti-roll bar complete the front suspension, along with rack-and-pinion steering that's new. What's more, this steering has a leading-arm layout, with the rack ahead of the wheel centerline, contributing some compliance understeer rather than a trailing arm's tendency of invoking oversteer under heavy lateral load. The Z51 steering has a quick 13.0:1 ratio and 2.0 turns lock-to-lock; the base steering is 15.5:1 and requires 2.4 turns of the wheel. Also, though the export Corvette comes with Z51, it gets the slower steering as part of the handling setup with those identical-width wheels front and rear.

The rear suspension has its share of beautifully forged alloy as well. It's a 5-link design, counting two trailing links, a lower lateral link, another behind it for toe adjustment and the half-shaft itself. The transverse FRP leaf spring, tube shocks and another anti-roll bar complete things back here.

The shocks, though, deserve special mention because they were in a process of change during our testing. For the first few months of actual production, the Z51 suspension came with conventional shocks, valved more ➤➤➤

firmly than those of the base suspension. Our test car, however, was fitted with the Bilstein gas-over shocks that are now coming off the assembly line in Z51-equipped cars.

We were mightily impressed with the new Corvette's Z51 suspension and two numbers will show you why: 63.8 (as in mph through our slalom) and 0.896 (as in g around our skidpad). To put these in perspective, note that only three cars in recent memory have bettered this slalom speed on street tires, the Renault Turbo, Ferrari 512 BB and Lamborghini Countach. And the Corvette's skidpad sets a new street-tire record, beating the Countach's 0.869g by a significant margin.

To amplify on these cold objective numbers, we can report that the Corvette's handling is a delight! Gone is the previous version's overshoot steering that caused you to uncrank some lock as the car took its set. You point this new Corvette and it goes. In fact, Corvette engineers showed us how they've gone to great lengths studying and quantifying the new car's yaw behavior; non-technically, what happens when you quickly twist the wheel. They offered graphs galore comparing it with other high performance cars.

Now you'd be surprised, of course, if Chevrolet data showed its new car to be inferior; and, needless to note, this isn't the case. But what's interesting is how well the company's comparative testing correlates with our two quantifications of handling, slalom and skidpad. Based on measurements of transient response time, maximum lateral acceleration, yaw frequency response and other engineeringese, Corvette folks place their own new car as best, with a close grouping of Porsche 944, Ferrari 308 and Porsche 928 next, followed by the Datsun 280ZX. Our slalom and skidpad numbers are, respectively, Corvette 63.8/0.896, Porsche 944 60.9/0.818, Ferrari 308GTSi 60.6/0.810, Porsche 928 59.7/0.810 and Datsun 280ZX Turbo 58.6/0.754.

Continuing with our own evaluations, we can report that the Corvette's tires and suspension give excellent communication of those VR50s doing your bidding, though the tires are rarely heard in protest. In fact, the skidpad's near-0.9g profited from *not* overworking the front tires. A bit less throttle, a little less steering input and concomitantly less understeer gave the best times. Through the slalom, our driver found that the impressive grip and excellent steering gave him two options, a smooth tight line or a little throttle-induced toss-and-catch; the former proved quicker, however.

The car's off-throttle transition (its "drop-throttle" behavior, as Corvette engineers call it) was exemplary in helping point the

car (or saving you if a curve tightened up unexpectedly). Nor was this new Corvette especially embarrassed by deteriorated road surfaces. The tires' communication level increased, all the better to tell you something had changed down there. And there was no mistaking the occasional feeling of fiberglass over steel (no, this new Corvette, though considerably better than the previous version, isn't carved from a solid block of anything). But much to its benefit, our Z51 displayed none of the chiropractic chagrin of the older Corvette's slalom suspension, even when the roads got particularly pock-marked.

And if speed needs to be dissipated in a hurry (i.e., your detector goes off), there's no problem because the Corvette's vented discs front and rear are every bit as impressive as its handling. New aluminum caliper assemblies from Girlock (a joint effort of Girling and Lockheed in Australia) feature a separation of clamping force and torque reaction, brought off via finite element analysis of caliper deformation under load. Semi-metallic brake pads sourced in Japan are also Corvette-unique.

And all of this new hardware performs, with panic stops from 60 mph in an amazingly short 133 ft, 80–0 in 250 ft, and so little fade in six 0.5g stops from 60 that we report it as "nil." The Corvette's brakes displayed only two shortcomings to our eyes (our right foot, actually): At only 16 lb for a 0.5g stop (a deceleration rate roughly midway between a gentle braking and an all-out panic), their pedal pressure was lighter than we prefer. Also, though fore/aft balance was very good, the brake pedal proved relatively insensitive to modulation as one or another tire probed lockup.

We've stopped and cornered this new Corvette. Now let's examine what makes it go. Move inboard from the rear suspension, if you will, and you'll see another elegantly shaped piece of aluminum on which rides the differential (of limited-slip variety with the Z51 option). Within are gears giving a 3.31:1 ratio for said Z51, other final drives giving 3.07:1 and a CAFE-motivated 2.73:1. Move forward and you'll find an aluminum alloy propshaft that resides in yet another piece of aluminum, a C-channel connecting the differential to the rear of the gearbox. The point of this backbone drivetrain is at least twofold: elimination of two crossmembers (allowing a lower seating package) and spreading the torque reaction over a greater length (permitting somewhat softer mounts for better drivetrain isolation).

The frame of the new Corvette is a spot-welded skeletal structure, as opposed to the previous arc-welded ladder frame. Attachment of the fiberglass body is via bonding or bolting; the backbone drivetrain is mounted from below.

This brings us to the gearbox in a roundabout way; and even here the new Corvette has something innovative to offer: a 4-speed + 3 OD. You read that correctly: four forward speeds plus three more in overdrive. The basic gearbox design was known as a Borg-Warner T-10, though its rights and tooling are now owned by Doug Nash (of Nash 5-speed fame). At the rear of the conventional 4-speed is a Nash-designed planetary gear set that reduces the direct drive ratios by 0.67. Now a little exercise with your handy calculator will confirm the adjacent figures and a trifle redundancy in the resulting concoction.

Gear	Ratio	Overdrive
1st	2.88:1	1.93:1
2nd	1.91:1	1.28:1
3rd	1.33:1	0.89:1
4th	1.00:1	0.67:1

Not true, though, because it's all under the control of a computer sensing engine speed, road speed, shift lever position and throttle angle. Also, the computer's smart enough to know 1st OD is almost spot-on with 2nd direct, so it dispenses with 1st OD entirely. As for the rest, think of having a conventional 4-speed under the control of your right hand, with each overdrive ratio having an automatic kickdown under the control of your right foot. And, because you're an enthusiast, you'd like absolute predictability when you're really into it, right? So once 2nd direct or 3rd direct is invoked by a playful right foot, the com-

SCALE: 10 in. (254 mm) DIVISIONS

PRICE

List price $23,360
Price as tested $24,705
    Price as tested includes std equip (air cond, elect. window lifts, elect. adj mirrors, anti-theft), AM/FM stereo/cassette ($895), elect. adj driver's seat ($210), Bilstein shock absorbers ($189), Z51 susp pkg ($51)

MANUFACTURER

Chevrolet Motor Div, General Motors Corp, 30007 Van Dyke Ave, Warren, Mich. 48090

GENERAL

Curb weight, lb/kg	3200	1455
Test weight	3450	1568
Weight dist (with driver), f/r, %		51/49
Wheelbase, in./mm	96.2	2444
Track, front/rear	59.6/60.4	1513/1534
Length	176.5	4483
Width	71.0	1804
Height	46.7	1186
Ground clearance	5.0	127
Overhang, f/r	40.5/39.8	1030/1009
Trunk space, cu ft/liters	11.6	328
Fuel capacity, U.S. gal./liters	20.0	76

ACCOMMODATION

Seating capacity, persons		2
Head room, in./mm	35.5	902
Seat width	2 x 20.0	2 x 508
Seatback adjustment, deg		12

ENGINE

Type		ohv V-8
Bore x stroke, in./mm	4.00 x 3.48	101.6 x 88.4
Displacement, cu in./cc	350	5733
Compression ratio		9.0:1
Bhp @ rpm, SAE net/kW	205/153 @ 4300	
Equivalent mph / km/h		140/225
Torque @ rpm, lb-ft/Nm	290/393 @ 2800	
Equivalent mph / km/h		92/148
Fuel injection		GM Throttle Body
Fuel requirement		unleaded, 91-oct

Exhaust-emission control equipment: 3-way catalytic converter with oxygen sensor, exhaust-gas recirculation, air injection

DRIVETRAIN

Transmission .... automatic; lockup torque converter with 4-sp planetary gearbox

Gear ratios: 4th (0.70)	2.32:1
3rd (1.00)	3.31:1
2nd (1.63)	5.40:1
1st (3.06)	10.13:1
1st (3.06 x 1.85)	18.74:1
Final drive ratio	3.31:1

INSTRUMENTATION

Instruments: 85-mph speedo (with digital display), 6000-rpm tach (with digital display), 99,999.9 odo, oil press./temp, coolant temp/voltmeter, fuel level, mpg, trip odo/range, clock
Warning lights: oil press., oil temp, coolant temp, alternator, brake sys, choke, security, check engine, low fuel, hatch ajar, door ajar, seatbelts, hazard, high beam, directionals

CHASSIS & BODY

Layout .... front engine/rear drive
Body/frame .... fiberglass body on skeletal steel chassis
Brake system .... 11.5-in. (292-mm) vented discs front & rear; vacuum assisted
  Swept area, sq in./sq cm 330 2128
Wheels .... cast alloy, 16 x 8½ front, 16 x 9½ rear
Tires .... Goodyear Eagle VR50, P255/50VR-16
Steering type .... rack & pinion, power assisted
  Overall ratio 13.0:1
  Turns, lock-to-lock 2.0
  Turning circle, ft/m .... 40.1 .... 12.2
Front suspension: unequal-length A-arms, transverse fiberglass leaf spring, tube shocks, anti-roll bar
Rear suspension: upper & lower trailing arms, lateral arms, tie rods, halfshafts, transverse fiberglass leaf spring, tube shocks, anti-roll bar

MAINTENANCE

Service intervals, mi:	
Oil/filter change	7500/15,000
Chassis lube	7500
Tuneup	30,000
Warranty, mo/mi	12/12,000

CALCULATED DATA

Lb/bhp (test weight)	16.8
Mph/1000 rpm (4th gear)	32.4
Engine revs/mi (60 mph)	1850
Piston travel, ft/mi	1075
R&T steering index	0.80
Brake swept area, sq in./ton	191

ROAD TEST RESULTS

ACCELERATION

Time to distance, sec:
0–100 ft	3.1
0–500 ft	8.3
0–1320 ft (¼ mi)	15.5
Speed at end of ¼ mi, mph	88.0

Time to speed, sec:
0–30 mph	2.4
0–60 mph	7.1
0–80 mph	12.6
0–100 mph	22.3

SPEEDS IN GEARS

4th (4200 rpm)	137
3rd (5200)	110
2nd (5200)	72
1st (4650)	34

FUEL ECONOMY

Normal driving, mpg .... est 18.0

HANDLING

Lateral accel, 100-ft radius, g 0.896
Speed thru 700-ft slalom, mph 63.8

BRAKES

Minimum stopping distances, ft:
From 60 mph	133
From 80 mph	250

Control in panic stop .... excellent
Pedal effort for 0.5g stop, lb 16
Fade: percent increase in pedal effort to maintain 0.5g deceleration in 6 stops from 60 mph .... nil
Parking: hold 30% grade? .... na
Overall brake rating .... excellent

INTERIOR NOISE

Idle in neutral, dBA	60
Maximum, 1st gear	80
Constant 30 mph	70
50 mph	74
70 mph	76
90 mph	80

SPEEDOMETER ERROR

30 mph indicated is actually	30.0
60 mph	60.0
80 mph	80.0

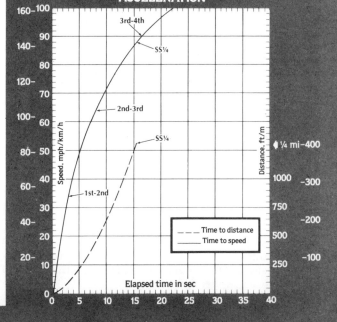

ACCELERATION

puter forgets overdrive regardless of throttle angle, provided you continue to play in 2nd or 3rd. A heavy-footed upshift to 4th will retain direct, but if you lift off or reach 110 mph, whichever arrives first, the computer snags 4th OD for you. Cruising the highway in top cog, you come to treat this gearbox just like an automatic with a kickdown mode for passing. And cruising around town, there's still enough acceleration to get yourself noticed by the local blues, even in 2nd, 3rd or 4th OD that comes automatically with light throttle.

Several journalists, particularly the foreign contingent, objected to the computer's controlling interest in this gearbox's business. They (and we) were interested to hear that export cars will have an overdrive on/off switch under driver control, and since that press introduction Chevrolet has also received clearance from the EPA to include it for the home market. At first there were doubts that it would be allowed; after all, we irresponsible drivers out there in the real world just might not be content to let the computer do all the thinking for us, might deviate from approved EPA driving procedures.

The test car in this report had not the 4+3 OD transmission, but rather the much more familiar 4-speed Turbo Hydra-matic that was standard in the Corvette in 1982. That's because the 4+3 was not released for production at the beginning of the model year. So we drove a 4+3 Corvette later, and our report on that follows.

The automatic is essentially the same as last year's, which is to say CAFE-calibrated via a lockup converter under the influence of a gentle right foot and well optimized for hot-shoe enjoyment if influences lead you in the other direction.

Continuing our trip up the Corvette's drivetrain brings us to another of the rare elements not justifying an "all-new," the trusty 350-cu.-in. V-8. Updated in last year's car, this engine features Cross Fire Injection (via GM Throttle Body) and an Electronic Control Module taking care of this fuel dosage as well as the spark. ECM also handles knock-sensed retardation of said spark and oxygen-sensed feeding of the catalytic converter downstream. Thus jazzed up, this V-8 seems to have reached the limits of its clean-air power: 205 bhp at 4300 rpm and 290 lb-ft of torque at 2800. We wouldn't be surprised to see port injection as its next refinement, maybe in the 1985 version (remember, this is a 1984 here). And there's more than just idle talk about an aluminum block.

Not that this Corvette is lacking in power, mind. We recorded a foot-stomping 7.1 seconds to 60 mph, burbled through the quarter mile in 15.5 sec at 88.0 mph and saw 100 mph in only 22.3 sec. Yet the Corvette engineer along for the day apologized for the car being on the slow side of the spectrum, what with its previous Riverside flogging and all. It certainly felt quick to us, though we did sense just a tad of overzealous spark retardation at the upper end of the rpm range. Later, we saw the same car come very close to its 4300-rpm bhp peak in 4th, 4200 to be precise and evidence of a 137-mph top speed.

Indeed, you get more than one bit of evidence of the speed you're going in the new Corvette, along with lots of other informational displays. Having chased technicalities from tire print to throttle body, let's sit for awhile and look around the cockpit. This is all-new as well, with many positive attributes and only a couple of downers to our mind.

It's a cockpit quite different from previous Corvettes. Gone, for instance, is the feeling of driver and passenger slipped into a pair of 13AAA shoes. The shapes (and actual dimensions as well) give an impression of broad expanses, much like the Camaro/Firebird layout. In fact, a couple of us accused the surfaces, finishes and overall aura of being excessively F-car, though Chevrolet copped the plea by reason of pilot-car configuration: 'Tis said graining and texturing of the plastic and vinyl come later in the parts-qualification process. The jury is still out.

And we're a hung jury as to instrumentation, several of us dogmatically convinced it's guilty of indecent digital exposure. Directly ahead of the driver is a collection of digital and digital/analog hybrid displays, multifunctions of which are controlled by switches on the center panel. Options include one readout combining oil pressure or temperature, another for coolant temperature or battery voltage, a third for instantaneous or average mpg (the latter indicating 15.7 after our Engineering Editor's drive) and a fourth giving trip odometer or range. There's yet another option: turning all four off and leaving only the bargraph fuel gauge, speedometer and tach. And choice of English or metric units at the flip of a switch could well become the best metric education device since the dollar bill. Even the digital-temperance fuddy-duddies among us appreciated the wealth of information provided by these displays.

Our objection, though, arises from those critical displays of continuously important information—the speedometer and tach. Each is a rectangle containing both digital and hybrid readouts, the latter through a stylized little multicolor horsepower curve for the tach and an arc representing 0–85 mph for the speedo. Curiously enough, the speedo's digital readout continues on up to the car's maximum speed, but we doubt the hybrid has sufficient arc length to display this expanded scale adequately. In any event, we'd prefer an optional gauge package for those of us evidently deficient in character recognition.

On another matter entirely, the seats of the new Corvette are exemplary in their comfort and support, particularly if one opts for the electrically adjustable driver's seat developed for the car by Lear Siegler. The base seat, of Chevrolet Conteur design, is very nice as well; but we can't imagine the shape of someone unable to become at one with the optional version. Buttons located at the front of either bolster and in the center console control fore/aft, height, cushion rake, seatback rake, lateral support and lumbar support, the penultimate through bolster angle of the cushion and seatback and the last via three electrically inflated bladders. Pump up one's own lumbar support with a sphygmomanometer bulb? How *passé*.

The view forward is influenced by the hood's subtle double bubble; and there's no claustrophobia to either side or rearward because of the relatively thin B-pillars and broad expanse of wraparound hatch. Adequate mirrors remove lane changes from the Hazardous Activities list and, as before, the inside mirror is one of those wide-angle jobs that makes the cars behind look particularly purposeful.

If the car following happens to be a new Corvette, it looks especially so. Styling experts have likened the new Corvette to the Ferrari 308 and, at another extreme, the Mazda RX-7, but never being ones to leave it to the experts, here's our view.

To a man and woman, we all admired the new Corvette's lines. They're clean, free of gimmicks, and they update the Corvette's image without completely redefining it. Notice how FRP capabilities are exploited so well. The clamshell hood tilts forward from a natural body break. This seam to the rear is covered by a single thin rub strip. And new technology of in-mold urethane coating gives a better finish so there's a chance of FRP painted surfaces matching the urethane endcaps front and rear.

Those of us who enjoy open-air motoring appreciate the lift-off roof panel, available in opaque (base) or see-through (optional) form. And those who are into structural integrity point out that this targa top is bolted in place, not simply latched.

There's a great deal of thoughtful design evident in this new Corvette, quite enough to bring it to the attention of those who felt the previous versions had become increasingly tacky. Is it now the best exotic car in the world? The best exotic car value?

This introductory road test left us wondering just how the new Corvette would stack up against the world's leading sports cars—machinery like the Porsche 928S and Ferrari 308GTBi. So as soon as we could, we got it together with those, plus the supposedly more humble Porsche 944.

Our report on that comparison test is in this *Guide*. And as you'll see, what we concluded from the experience described here was not exactly the same as what we found when the 1984 Corvette was pitted against the international elite. ◨

10

Corvette muscles in

We drive the European version of this great American sports car

By Bob Cooke

THE EASY power of that 5.7-litre V8 says it all. Cruising at 120 mph is no problem; nor is getting up to that cruising speed. None of that frenetic, wheel-spinning, gear-snatching that characterises some European sporting cars, just a dull, competent roar from those twin huge tailpipes and those wide, low-profile tyres eat up the scenery.

We old-worlders talk glibly of the "Europeanisation" of American cars, but when you talk to Dave McLellan, the guy who engineered the new Corvette, you realise that Americans don't really give much of a damn for European standards. The Corvette is smaller, lighter, better riding and better handling than any previous American muscle car, but not because of anything we Europeans may want: the new 'Vette is still all apple pie. Nor do you get the impression that GM are particularly worried about foreign competition eating into the US sports car market. The Datsun Z-cars and the Mazda RX7 did not eat into the market so much as expand it, says McLellan; the sort of affluent young man who has traditionally bought Corvettes is still buying them, and GM are gambling on the chance that the post-war baby boom generation which is now reaching maturity will in fact increase the Corvette share of the market, and they're talking of producing 37,000 or so a year.

Some of that production will be offered for sale in Europe, with first models appearing in showrooms in June. To achieve type certification for European countries there had to be some sops to European requirements, but these have been limited to revised electrical systems, lighting, glass, mirrors and metric instrumentation. The European version has the uprated "Z51" handling package (that means firmer, handling-oriented suspension) and four-speed overdrive automatic transmission. Because in European trim GM can drop the catalytic converter in the exhaust system, this is being replaced with a resonator; also, because of the heavier traffic conditions and different patterns of usage in Europe an oil cooler is a standard fitting. To meet the laws there are towing hooks front and rear, revised rear panel to accept larger licence plates, louder horn and breakaway door mirrors.

But the Corvette is still very American. "There's no way we want to change the character of the Corvette," says McLellan. "We couldn't possibly have fitted, say, a V6. That 200 horse power, 350 cu.in. V8 is what Corvette is all about."

So the Corvette goes all right, but does it handle? Think American and you do tend to think of wallow, of suspension tuned for comfort on long highway cruises rather than for taut handling over the sort of winding, country roads that so appeal to the European driver. In this sense the new Corvette is something of an eye-opener. Suspension is firm without being harsh, cornering ability is exceptional and handling is quirk-free and thoroughly predictable. The rack and pinion steering is power assisted, but is remarkably direct allowing the car to be placed accurately through cornering; straight-line stability is excellent.

Thrashing a European spec Corvette round the Goodyear tyre company's test circuit near Luxembourg gave us an ideal opportunity to put GM's claims for the Corvette's roadholding and handling to the test. They appear to be eminently justified. The Corvette was "real fun" to drive, exhibiting moderate understeer in corners taken at speeds approaching the very high limits of adhesion, with no quirky behaviour if, for instance, the driver lifts off suddenly in mid-curve. However, if deliberately provoked the Corvette would willingly hang out its tail, where it could be held for spectacular steady state oversteer cornering or quickly brought back into line. GM claim the Corvette has the best cornering ability of any production car, being able to maintain 0.95g lateral force in standard condition. Much of the credit for this exceptional performance is given to Goodyear, who achieved a remarkable combination of requirements in the Eagle 255/50VR16 tyres developed specially for the Corvette. They met all GM's demands, which were for fuel-saving low rolling resistance plus high grip (normally contradictory factors in tyre design), fast heat dissipation, low road noise, good wet traction. Tyre and suspension design developed hand in hand

over three years, leading eventually to an evidently successful compromise combining low profile tyres and sports suspension without the expected harshness of ride; limited body roll and braced tread edges help to keep the full tread pattern in contact with the road under all conditions, not only improving traction but contributing to extended tyre life, even with sustained hard driving.

Lacking our test gear, we were unable to check GM's claims of 140 mph top speed. McLellan commented, however, that the Corvette's electronic, digital-readout speedometer gives pretty accurate results, since it reads pulses from the transmission output. Going by that, we were doing a true 120 mph at the end of the Goodyear test track's one-mile straight before having to brake for the adverse camber curve at the end. And that beefy motor hadn't yet run out of puff. Acceleration was impossible to check because the electronic speedometer updates only at half-second intervals, all right for general use but not for the accuracy we demand.

The Corvette's roof comes off easily and stows in the back under the large glass tailgate. Driving with the roof off

dramatically increases wind noise, but there is little buffeting inside the cockpit. Air seems to sweep well over occupants' heads, but strikes the frame behind, setting up a fairly noisy roar. But then we were doing 110 mph. . . .

Although GM are experimenting with different wheel widths front and rear – the mainstream US version will have 8in. fronts and 8½in. rears, while another could have 9in. rears – the version for Europe has 8in. wheels front and rear.

GM have no plans to market the Corvette in Britain, partially because a right-hand-drive version is physically impractical without resiting the engine.

Left: On the Goodyear test track the 1984 Corvette proved easy to keep in line, easy to provoke into a tail-out slide if required. Fun to drive with no quirks, and good adhesion wet or dry

Wheel and tyre show unidirectional features clearly. Tyre tread follows F1 wet tyre pattern aimed at ducting water out of tyre's footprint as quickly as possible. Yet in spite of knobbly look noise is restrained

Corvette uses AC (the spark plug people, a GM division) electronic instrument cluster. LCD displays show speed, engine rpm and fuel contents; speed and rpm are shown in digital and analog bar graph form

THE NEW CORVETTE

Back On Top—With Performance Figures to Back It Up

By Marlan Davis

What would you pay for a car that had the following: fully independent front and rear suspension with mostly aluminum components, 13:1 rack-and-pinion power steering, four-wheel disc brakes with aluminum calipers, speed-rated radial tires with a trick directional tread pattern and 16-inch aluminum wheels, tilt "clamshell" hood, halogen driving lights, 4-speed manual trans (backed by an electric 2-speed overdrive) or 4-speed automatic overdrive trans, aluminum differential with aluminum propshaft and halfshafts, digital/tape display instrumentation with

"Never underestimate America—or General Motors."

computer diagnostic callouts, six-way adjustable electric driving seat, high-tech stereo system, 140 mph top speed, and .95 G cornering ability as delivered from the factory? $50,000? $75,000? $100,000? After all, the description sounds like a Ferrari, Lamborghini, or perhaps a Porsche, and they're all priced way up there. We all know only foreign cars have all those neat parts, right?

Sorry. Never underestimate America—or General Motors. For this car is built right here in Bowling Green, Kentucky, and will probably cost only $25,000 to $30,000. It's called the "New Corvette," and you should be seeing it in your dealer show room by the end of March. This car is among the best handling production cars the world has seen, thanks to both the genius of Chevrolet Engineering and the

radical new P255/50VR-16 Goodyear tires that feature a unique tread pattern requiring separate right and left-hand tires.

I had an opportunity to drive this fantastic new car at the famous Riverside road racing course, and it's a much better car than most of us are drivers. Once, I took the wrong line setting up for the infamous "S-turns," and felt I was "in a heap o' trouble now, boy." In desperation, I yanked the wheel in what I thought was a hopeless attempt to stay on the pavement, but the car went through the series of turns faster than I'd ever gone before, without so much as a twitch. More experienced drivers report the car is as fast as many all-out race cars around the course, including Formula Ford open wheelers. Brake fade? Forget it; in fact, they and the tires are so good you can go in a corner so deep it'll scare you. I think one of Chevy's RPOs (Regular Production Options) should be "Driving Skill," so the owner can learn to use the car to the full extent of its capabilities.

"This car is among the best handling production cars the world has seen . . ."

Everything about the car—front to rear—is revolutionary. Perhaps the styling is not as radical as some anticipated, but the car's simple, clean lines perfectly illustrate the "form follows function" philosophy, having only a .34 drag coefficient. The entire hood pivots forward, providing easy access to all engine and front suspension compo-

The body may be all new, but you can still tell it's a Vette. Note the concealed headlamps, front fender vents, subtle rear spoiler, and big round taillights (which is what most non-Vette owners will be seeing the most of). All Vettes will have an electrically actuated hatchback, one piece lift-off top, and a readily accessible engine compartment, thanks to the trick clamshell hood.

When you lean on this car, it just doesn't lean—note the absence of body roll in the turns. Chevrolet reports that the Z51 handling package can generate .95 G on the skidpad in production form with full tread on the tires, and more than 1 G if the owner was to install the 9½-inch wheels up front and modify the alignment settings. Even the base car can generate .87. There is only one "stock" production car that's better—the BMW M1 can hit 1G—but it ought to, for $100,000-plus. Ferrari, Porsche, Lamborghini, and Maserati are all below .87!

CORVETTE

A computer-controlled 2-speed automatic overdrive unit backs up the traditional Super T-10 4-speed. Clutch linkage is now hydraulically actuated.

nents. On its underside are built-in ducts that take cold air from ahead of the radiator and force feed it to the fuel-injected engine. There's still a lift-off roof, but it's now a single panel that eliminates the old T-bar. And, yes, there's a hatchback—electrically actuated by any of three different switches, of course. Overall width has been increased 2 inches, resulting in wider front and rear track, as well as added interior space. Other exterior dimensions were reduced, which, when com-

"Everything about the car—front to rear—is revolutionary."

bined with the extensive use of aluminum chassis parts, reduces weight by about 250 pounds compared to the '82 model. This results in a 20 mpg combined EPA city/highway mileage figure for the automatic-transmissioned cars . . . and allows the retention of the big 350-cubic-inch engine.

The engine/trans combination itself is rigidly attached to the differential by a C-shaped aluminum crossbeam that both reduces overall frame weight and provides additional interior room through the elimination of the trans and differential crossmembers. What remains of the traditional perimeter frame utilizes high-strength steel only where necessary to reduce weight. Aluminum extensions support the rear bumper.

The familiar front coil springs were replaced by a revolutionary "intelligent" transverse fiberglass monoleaf spring that is lighter, more durable, and actually able to differentiate between jounce and roll due to its method of support—two fulcrum points one-third of the way in from each end of the spring. Under normal highway cruising conditions, the spring flexes in a bent "V" motion (much like a bow and arrow) over normal bumps and irregularities, yet when the car is pushed to the limit in a turn and the chassis starts to roll (with one side of the chassis falling and the other rising), the spring twists into an "S" shape, thereby increasing its effective rate (and hence roll stiffness) about 20 percent. This lets the car get by with only a 25mm sway bar (by contrast the Z28 uses a 32mm bar), thus offering a marked ride quality improvement.

The aluminum front A-arms are offset, with the lower A-arm located considerably ahead of the upper arm, in turn also slightly offsetting the aluminum spindle. When combined with a +3 percent

caster setting, this allows the tire, as it transitions through a turn, to have the desired negative camber, but without the excessive tire scrub and/or sluggishness on steering wheel response normally associated with high-caster settings. The new car's roll center is also quite high for a production car, the body exhibiting little roll in the corners.

Out back, a new five-link independent rear suspension helps end the twitchiness associated with the Vette rearend, reducing lateral force compliance while providing good understeer characteristics. The knuckles and upper and lower control arms on all the new Vettes are aluminum, as are the driveshaft and half-shafts on manual trans-equipped cars (and with the automatic when the power driving seat and/or heavy-duty suspension is ordered). The 16-inch wheels are 1 inch wider in the rear than up front; this allows the rear tires to work harder before breaking traction, enhancing handling by increasing directional control and lateral stability. There are separate right and left-hand wheels, made necessary by the uniquely shaped cooling fins.

The car's most controversial aspect is its unique manual trans setup. It's still a Super T-10 4-speed, but now it's backed by a computer-controlled overdrive that automatically shifts into overdrive under pre-programmed part throttle operating conditions to maximize fuel

"Inside, it's like you're in an F16."

economy, as well as cutting in at speeds in excess of 112 mph. Overdrive is said to be automatically overridden at speeds below 112 mph under high-pressure driving conditions, but we did experience some unexpected kickdowns, and sometimes in a hard 4th-to-3rd gear downshift there was some slight gear clash. A manual lockout that bypasses the computer is really needed and said to be easily installable, but Chevrolet could not do it because of the government-mandated fuel economy standards. But that doesn't stop us hot rodders, does it? (Rumor has it that cars destined for Canada may eventually get a manual lockout, in which case it will simply be a matter of going down to the local dealer and ordering parts.)

Because of the wide tires and large 9½-inch rear wheels, a hydraulic clutch is used to reduce drivetrain loading during speed shifting. This, apparently, did not affect shift quality during acceleration runs.

Would you believe it—stock aluminum finned calipers. They're made by Girlock in Australia, and the car brakes so well it's uncanny.

Cooling is handled by an aluminum-cored radiator with plastic side tanks, and the radiator support is made from bubble-filled fiberglass, again to reduce weight. A single serpentine belt drives all engine accessories, while the traditional engine-driven fan is replaced by an electric unit that operates only as needed at speeds below 35 mph.

Inside, it's like you're in an F16. An on-board computer provides digital readouts of range and instant and average miles per gallon. Warning signals alert the driver to low fuel supply, high engine oil and water temp, and low oil pressure and voltage. As before, the speedometer and tach dominate the area in front of the driver, but now read out both as a tape display and digitally. The digital speedo tops out at more than 140; the tach's tape display follows the engine's dyno horsepower trace curve.

Meanwhile, there's probably 50 percent of you out there who still want to pop *the question*, namely, "Never mind this G-whiz, what'll it do in the quarter?" Well, we haven't yet had the opportunity to run one through at the drags, but Chevy says the automatic will run 15.1s with no sweat, and the manual is several tenths quicker. Hopefully, we'll soon be getting a Vette of our own to try out and verify these figures. Besides, *I* want one. Anybody got $25,000 to loan a poor, impoverished staff writer? Oh, so you thought they just gave them to us . . . . **HR**

This new five-link rear suspension really keeps those rear tires firmly planted on the ground through the most severe cornering maneuvers. Most components are aluminum. A rear sway bar is now standard equipment. This unique "backbone" supports the trans and differential carrier, eliminating the traditional crossmembers. Result: improved interior space and weight saving to boot since the external perimeter frame can be lightened somewhat.

Up front, the A-arms and spindles are made from forged aluminum. The arms are offset, improving the car's anti-dive characteristics (that means the nose doesn't dip under braking). Coil springs were replaced with a more durable and effective transverse fiberglass-reinforced plastic leaf spring. GM and Goodyear worked together for more than two years to develop the unique directional-tread tire, which has a tread pattern similar to the Formula One rain tires. Regardless of the turn's direction, the tire's shoulder grooves work with the car, instead of against it; separate right and left-hand tires are required. Handling is unsurpassed, wet or dry, but there's still decent ride quality, and a special layer of rubber under the tread enhances fuel efficiency. Because of the unique cooling fins and wider diameter rear wheels, there are four separate 16-inch wheels required, one for each corner.

All gauges are tape display and/or digital readout, backed by emergency warning signals. The unique steering wheel lets you see all the gauges all the time.

New Corvette Specifications

(As we went to press, Chevrolet was unsure whether the car is to be considered an '83 or '84 model, due to the lateness of its introduction.)

Engine

Engine Type .... 90-degree OHV V8
Cubic Inches/Liters... 350/5.7
Bore x Stroke .... 4.00 x 3.48 inches
Induction .... Cross-fire (twin throttle body) single point, pulse-type electronic fuel injection
Compression Ratio ... 9.0:1
Horsepower .... 205 net hp @ 4300 rpm
Torque .... 290 lbs.-ft. @ 2800 rpm
Fuel Type .... Unleaded (engine has automatic knock-sensing timing retard)

Driveline

Transmissions:

Manual ...... Super T-10 4-speed, with computer-controlled OD in 2nd, 3rd, and 4th gears; ratios, without OD: 2.88/1.91/1.33/1.00; with .67 OD: 2.88/1.28/.89/.67

Automatic...700R4 4-speed OD with high-stall torque converter, ratios: 3.06/1.63/1.00/.70

Rearend .... Dana 36 carrier with 7⅞-inch ring-and-pinion; final drive ratio: 3.31 standard, 3.55 optional

Suspension

Front .... Independent SLA design with fiberglass-reinforced plastic transverse dual-pivot leaf spring, unequal length upper and lower aluminum control arms, aluminum spindles, 24mm sway bar (25mm with Z51), direct double-acting Delco hydraulic shock absorbers (Bilstein gas shock absorbers scheduled as running change on Z51)

Rear .... Five-link fully independent with fixed aluminum differential, upper and lower longitudinal control arms, U-jointed wheel drive shafts (aluminum on some cars; see text), lateral strut, steering tie rod, fiberglass-reinforced transverse leaf spring, 20mm rear sway bar, direct double-acting Delco shock absorbers (Bilstein gas shocks scheduled as running change on Z51)

Steering .... Power rack-and-pinion with standard tilt-and-telescopic steering wheel; 15.5:1 ratio, standard; 13.01:1 ratio, optional with Z51 handling package

Measurements

Turning Diameter (curb to curb) .... 40.1 inches, outside front; 25.0 inches, inside rear
Wheelbase .... 96.2 inches
Overall Length .... 176.5 inches
Overall Height .... 46.7 inches
Overall Width .... 71.0 inches
Tread (front/rear) .... 59.6/60.4 inches
Weight (std. equip.) ....3117 pounds
Weight Distribution (percent front/rear) 50.8/49.2
Fuel Capacity .... 20 gallons
Useable Cargo Space ...... 17.9 cubic feet
Tires
   Standard .... P215/65R-15 steel-belted radial*
   Optional .... P255/50VR-16 steel-belted Goodyear radial rated for 140 mph
Wheels .... Separate right/left hand

*As we went to press, it was reliably reported that the optional wheels and tires may be installed on all cars, with or without the Z51 package.

Under the hood, there's an injected 350. Note how the engine compartment has really been cleaned up. Everything is color-coordinated in gray and black. There are even T-handles on the dipsticks. All bracketry is aluminum, as is the radiator, water pump, and master cylinder. Can aluminum heads be far behind?

COMPARISON
R&T
ROAD TEST

A PERFORMANCE PAIR:

CHEVROLET

CORVETTE VS

NISSAN

300-ZX TURBO

America's answer to the Z-car takes on Japan's answer to the Vette

COMPARISON TESTS AT *Road & Track* arise in several ways. Sometimes it begins with soul searching to select the most suitable cars in a particular class. Other times, there's a benchmark car used to assess the strengths and weaknesses of a new competitor. Now and again, though, we're completely impulsive: "Hey, have you driven that new Glitzflib? Wow, does it ever knock the Smedley out of the water." Or, perhaps more thoughtfully, "You know, I'm struck by how similar those two are."

This comparison test falls into the last category. It just so happened that Chevrolet's 4+3 Overdrive Corvette and Nissan's 300-ZX Turbo arrived at our offices simultaneously. We drove them on the street, filled their notebooks, gathered our track data and, as we did, the collective impulse arose. Both cars are resplendent with features—and, at another level entirely, gimmicks; both are very quick in today's spectrum; both are recent updates of extremely successful predecessors; their dimensions, weights and overall feel are roughly comparable; and each had us asking, "How do you think this one compares with the other?"

"Set up a route and let's find out." The accompanying tables let you get up to speed on this, and the following comments give you a head start.

Though we've seen the 300-ZX in a couple of settings already (on the sly in August 1983; in Japan by November), this was our first opportunity to live with one for awhile on home ground. We chose the Turbo for said opportunity, which also implied at this point the 3-speed+ OD automatic. "Mixing apples and oranges?" you may say, what with the Vette's manual gearbox. Not really, and we refer you to the accompanying article on the Vette's 4+3 to learn just how smart a manual gearbox can be.

Ah, you're back. Let's continue our analysis of the two. Our Corvette had several elements not available at the time of our August 1983 "Four High Performance Cars" test; specifically, the aforementioned 4+3 Overdrive and a full-house Z51 suspension. The Z51 was of interest as our first experience with a production set of the Bilstein gas-over shocks, as fitted to our prototype Corvette test car (March 1983).

Each of our test cars was loaded with features such as cruise control, air conditioning, electric window lifts, AM/FM stereo/cassette, adjustable steering wheel (the ZX's, for rake; the Vette's, rake and reach), electrically adjustable mirrors (the Vette's are heated as well) and multi-multi-adjustable seats (the ZX's, manually; the Vette's driver seat, electrically but for seatback rake). As you can imagine, neither car lacked for creature comforts, with the Vette perhaps getting the apparent nod on paper, but the ZX more than holding its own in actual fact.

A Corvette has been traditionally upmarket of a Z-car in price, and this is still very much the case, especially when one starts fooling with the options list. Our 300-ZX Turbo's base price is $18,699 and, indeed, she goes for this as-tested, what

with all the items cited being standard equipment. By contrast, the Corvette's base of $23,360 rises to $26,210 as-tested, once one opts for the trick Delco-GM/Bose sound system ($895), transparent roof panel ($595), leather-faced seats ($400), electrical adjustment for the driver's seat ($210) and so on, down the list. Its suspension options deserve amplification as well: The Goodyear Eagle VR50 tires on their directionally finned wheels used to be a $561 option, but these are now standard on all Corvettes. Also, at prototype time, the Z51 suspension was slated to have the Bilsteins; early production Z51s didn't because the supply pipeline hadn't been established; and, at any rate, the latest plan is to separate the two: The Z51's stiffer springs and bars go for $51; the Bilsteins, an added $189. Did you follow all that?

Continuing this trend of the Corvette having more of things, including dollars invested, we can observe it has two more cylinders, three more forward speeds, 4.9 in. more wheelbase, 5.8 in. more overall length, 3.1 in. more width, 160 lb more curb weight and 2773 cc more displacement. This is getting silly. Invoke a 1.5 turbo equivalence and the displacement difference shrinks to 1293 cc; but, more to the point, the Corvette's 5.7-liter ohv V-8 produces 205 bhp and 290 lb-ft of torque whereas the 300-ZX's 3.0-liter turbocharged sohc V-6 is rated at 200 bhp and 227 lb-ft. Neither, we shall see, is lacking in oomph.

To confirm this and other relevant truths, four staff members took the cars on a 4-legged loop that gave each of us a bit of freeway, a fair number of desert whoop-de-dos—our Colorado Desert (strangely enough, located in California) is rarely flat, you realize—and also an extremely useful subloop that allowed each driver a direct back-to-back evaluation on precisely the same roads. Other elements of the drive included more than a little hillclimbing and some rather ordinary traffic-limited stuff. It was a Friday afternoon by then; everyone, including us, simply wanted to get home. Our Engineering Editor even passed up a used book store he'd never visited.

Along the way, we did an evaluation of 20 items, everything from engine to interior styling, luggage space and loading to quietness. As is our custom, we rated each of these on a scale of 1 (the pits) to 10 (the winner's circle). Also, after the trip each of us chose a personal favorite in two ways, price-dependent and in the Rich-Uncle mode. An accompanying table collects these subjective data; other tables compare objective matters of general information and performance.

More Power to Us All

THERE'S NO substitute for cubic inches, unless perhaps it's a turbo. "A great rumbling V-8 with gobs of torque," noted one driver. Need you ask which engine he was referring to? We all agreed that the Vette engine's only shortcoming was its relative unhappiness above 4000 rpm. Yet, as another driver noted, "With so much torque, who needs revs?" But we also lauded the excellent driveability, smooth power and exemplary mid-range punch of the 300-ZX. As one driver concluded, "I admire each of these powerplants, but for entirely different reasons."

Discussions of the transmissions generated similar views. We were (almost) unanimous in our appreciation of the Vette's 4+3. Indeed, even the single dissident didn't mind the gearbox—it was the linkage to which he objected. "So stiff and unwieldy," he said, "that it's a blessing some of the shifts are automatic." Others among us recalled how really horrid the typical muscle car shifter used to be, and gave the Vette a pat on the lever for improvement. In general, the more each of us drove the 4+3, the better we liked it. "This is utterly in keeping with the car's character," observed one driver, "because you can hulk that big gearbox around if you like, or just get by on torque if that's your wont."

In a similar vein, the ZX's 3-speed automatic+ OD was also in keeping with its character: smooth, unobtrusive, yet capable. Left in Drive, it shifts rather early, so several of us churned this gearbox around almost as much as we did the Vette's in spirited driving. We liked the OD lockout and, in fact, one driver observed, "This is what the Vette's automatic needs, so it won't hunt around at highway speeds." And with OD engaged, there is a striking similarity between the ZX's kickdown from OD to 3rd and the Vette's 4th OD to 4th direct. Either is admirably suited to highway passing conditions or simply to tug you reassuringly into that seat.

And either powertrain is admirably suited for giving you a quick run through the gears, though our instrumentation recognized that the Vette was just a tad quicker. It beat the ZX off the line, got to 60 in 7.1 seconds versus the ZX's 7.4, reached the quarter mile in 15.6 sec traveling 88.5 mph vs the ZX's 15.7 at 86.0 and continued to pull away, right up to its 136-mph top speed vs the ZX's 133. We'll make three observations about these figures: First, this particular 4+3 Vette is a bit slower than the previous automatic Vettes we've tested; second, the new ZX Turbo is uniformly quicker than the turbo Z-car it replaces; and, last, you'd have to be greedy indeed to want more straight-line performance than offered by either of these cars.

Getting a Grip on the Situation

Two vivid recollections sum up the differences of ride and handling with this pair. One is playing boy racer with the Vette, reaching absolutely astonishing limits of grip while it jiggles you to death on any but mirror-smooth roads. The other is playing suspension engineer with the ZX, as you fool with its cockpit-adjustable shock absorbers.

To take each in turn, the Vette's extremely firm suspension and super-wide tires make it benign almost to the point of dullness, provided the road surface is a good one. The car responds admirably to its steering, once you're accustomed to its quickness, but those desiring throttle control of attitude will be disappointed. "You steer this car to its limits," noted one driver, "you don't try to horse it around with the throttle." And these limits are high: We recorded a lateral acceleration of 0.880g around our skidpad and a slalom speed of 63.2 mph, the latter especially impressive when you consider the thought of weaving a 71.0-in. wide car through seven 100-ft gates.

Impressive grip on smooth surfaces, however, degrades into a darty feel as the road surface worsens. "This suspension doesn't just talk to me," said one staff member, "It yells." "It doesn't just yell," noted another, "it beats me about the head and shoulders." And this extremely poor ride ultimately affects the Vette's handling, steering feel, body structure, quietness and—we can't help conjecturing—long-range durability. There's a distinct feeling that the entire car is destined to

CALCULATED DATA		
	Chevrolet Corvette	Nissan 300-ZX Turbo
Lb/bhp (test weight)	16.7	16.0
Mph/1000 rpm (top gear)	36.7	26.1
Engine revs/mi (60 mph)	1650	2300
Piston travel, ft/mi	960	1250
R&T steering index	0.80	1.16
Brake swept area, sq in./ton	193	239

become one giant rattle in time.

This characteristic was confirmed another way in our sound measurements. For example, our readings with the Corvette at maximum 1st gear, constant 50 and constant 70 mph were 80, 73 and 77 dBA, respectively. These compare with the rather more plush ZX's 73, 68 and 73, implying, among other things, that the ZX is no louder at 6000 rpm in 1st or at 70 mph than the Vette is at 50. A boisterous V-8 conspired in this, although the Vette's stiff suspension and the resulting road noise were definitely part of the conspiracy as well.

Indeed, based on more than noise level, we concluded that the ZX exhibits a much better compromise of ride and handling. And you've got three such compromises at the flip of a console-mounted switch. Since prototype intro time, Nissan engineers have wisely broadened the spectrum of the ZX's adjustable shock control. Changes from soft to normal to firm now bring about distinctly different rides for different road conditions. For instance, we could trick ourselves into thinking that the soft setting miraculously erased freeway ripples. The firm setting, though a bit on the jiggly side, was still more comfortable than anything we experienced in the Vette. And, in general, subtle updates of the ZX's MacPherson-strut front/semi-trailing-arm rear suspension have lessened its tendency toward ultimate twitchiness. The car is still answerable to throttle, but now it's a virtue rather than a vice.

These subjective impressions were reinforced by our quantitative testing as well. The 300-ZX rounded our skidpad at 0.795g, up from 0.754g for the previous model. What's more, we recorded a slalom speed of 62.8 mph with the car on its firm shock setting, an impressive 4.2 mph quicker than the previous ZX's twitchy tour around the cones. Even on its soft setting, exhibiting a bit of the earlier car's nervousness, the new one could still maintain 60.3 mph.

These figures, you'll note, are inferior to the Corvette's. And, in fact, the smoother the road, the easier it was for our Vette pilot ⟫→

GENERAL DATA

	Chevrolet Corvette	Nissan 300-ZX Turbo
Base price	$23,360	$18,699
Price as tested[1]	$26,210	$18,699
Layout	front engine/rwd	front engine/rwd
Engine type	ohv V-8	turbo sohc V-6
Bore x stroke, mm	101.6 x 88.4	87.0 x 83.0
Displacement, cc	5733	2960
Compression ratio	9.0:1	7.8:1
Bhp @ rpm, SAE net	205 @ 4300	200 @ 5200
Torque @ rpm, lb-ft	290 @ 2800	227 @ 3600
Fuel injection	GM Throttle Body	Bosch L-Jetronic
Transmission	4-sp manual + 3-sp overdrive	3-sp automatic + overdrive
Gear ratios, :1	2.88	2.46
	1.91 (1.28)[2]	1.46
	1.33 (0.89)	1.00
	1.00 (0.67)	0.69
Final drive ratio, :1	3.07	3.70
Steering type	rack & pinion, power assisted	rack & pinion, power assisted
Brake system, f/r	11.5-in. vented discs, f & r	10.8-in. vented discs/ 11.4-in. discs
Wheels	cast alloy, 16 x 8½ f, 16 x 9½ r	cast alloy, 15 x 6½JJ
Tires	Goodyear Eagle VR50 P255/50VR-16	Goodyear Eagle GT, P215/60R-15
Suspension, f/r	unequal-length A-arms, transverse fiberglass leaf spring, tube shocks, anti-roll bar/ upper & lower trailing arms, tie rods, halfshafts, transverse fiberglass leaf spring, tube shocks, anti-roll bar	MacPherson struts, lower lateral arms, compliance struts, coil springs, tube shocks, anti-roll bar/ semi-trailing arms, coil springs, tube shocks, anti-roll bar

[1]Price as tested includes: For the Chevrolet Corvette, std equip (air conditioning, elect. window lifts, elect. adj mirrors, sport wheels & Eagle VR50 tires, adj steering wheel), Delco-GM/Bose AM/FM stereo/cassette ($895), transparent removable roof panel ($595), leather seating ($400), elect. adj driver seat ($210), Bilstein shocks ($189), cruise control ($185), central locking ($165), rear-window & mirror heat ($160), Z51 sus ($51); for the Nissan 300-ZX Turbo, std equip (air conditioning, elect. window lifts, elect. adj mirrors, AM/FM stereo/cassette, cruise control, remote-adj shocks, central locking).

[2]For the Chevrolet Corvette, gear ratios are direct (overdrive).

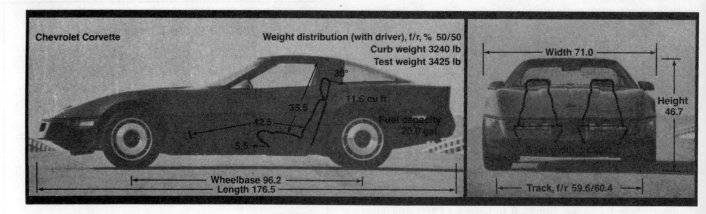

Chevrolet Corvette

Weight distribution (with driver), f/r, % 50/50
Curb weight 3240 lb
Test weight 3425 lb

30°
11.6 cu ft
35.5
42.5
5.5
fuel capacity
20.0 gal.

Wheelbase 96.2
Length 176.5

Width 71.0
Height 46.7

Track, f/r 59.6/60.4

of the hour to pull away from the ZX. On questionable surfaces, though, he bounced around while doing so, got less artful in his line and probably didn't enjoy himself very much. Though distinctly different in their behavior, these two cars aren't that far apart in usable grip and realizable manueverability when mixing it up in a less than perfectly paved world.

Braking behavior of both cars bordered on the phenomenal, though again, with meaningful contrast. In our panic stop evaluations, the Vette posted distances of 144 and 250 ft from 60 and 80 mph, respectively. The ZX bettered these, though insignificantly, with 141 and 249 ft. Both cars had exemplary fore/aft balance; nor did either display any fade to speak of in our 6-stops-from-60 routine. The differences came in how these two responded to heavy braking. The Corvette's firm suspension exhibited next to no brake dive; its pedal felt somewhat on the hard side and not especially amenable to modulation. By con-

trast, the ZX was softer overall; in pedal feel, in longitudinal pitch and even laterally. Its brake pedal had a spongy, longish travel that nonetheless proved extremely easy to modulate. Even with the firm shock setting, though, you'd think twice about heavy braking in a corner, for example.

Now Relax and Drive

YOU SIT low in a Corvette and, for that matter, in a ZX as well. Neither offers the unobstructed outward vision of an especially tall greenhouse; nor is either claustrophobic in any sense. Both cars feel bulky, however, no doubt because of their low seating and commensurately high cockpit sides.

In one sense, we've gotten used to the Corvette's vast array of digital and digital/analog hybrid graphics. Everyone appreciated the wealth of information that can be gleaned from the 3-mode display of coolant temperature/voltmeter, oil temperature/pres-

A GEARBOX SMARTER THAN YOUR AVERAGE DRIVER

WE WERE TANTALIZED by the Corvette's 4+3 Overdrive gearbox at the press introduction, and now we've had opportunity to put quite a few miles on a production Vette equipped with this innovative hardware.

As you may recall, it's a 4-speed manual gearbox combined with a Doug Nash-designed planetary gearset that applies a computer-controlled OD ratio of 0.67:1 to 2nd, 3rd and 4th cogs. Also, there has been a significant modification since the prototype intro; to wit, an OD lockout switch originally scheduled for Europe only has become a part of our setup as well.

How well does it work? To help you form an opinion, locate your handy calculator, examine the accompanying table of gear data and come along for an imaginary drive.

Gear	Direct, mph/1000 rpm	Overdrive, mph/1000 rpm
1st	8.6	none
2nd	13.0	19.5
3rd	18.4	27.6
4th	24.5	36.7

First, if you don't feel like learning anything just yet, then set the OD rocker switch to its off position. It's to your right on the center console, near the electric window and mirror controls. You're now driving a conventional 4-speed, though one with ratios that are unfashionably short these days—especially for a 350-cu-in. engine that's hardly rev-happy to begin with.

Ready to try the OD? Fine, flip the switch. Nothing happens? Not to worry,

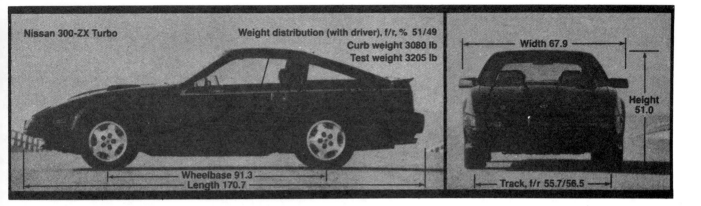

Nissan 300-ZX Turbo
Weight distribution (with driver), f/r, % 51/49
Curb weight 3080 lb
Test weight 3205 lb
Wheelbase 91.3
Length 170.7
Width 67.9
Height 51.0
Track, f/r 55.7/56.5

sure, instantaneous/average mpg and trip odometer/range (the third mode in each case being "off"). In fact, a couple of us brushed up on our English/SI knowledge by flipping yet another switch back and forth on the freeway stretches of our trip. But we'd still like to see blessedly conventional displays of mph and rpm. Two other points: Despite our general dislike of pure digital readouts for mph and rpm, we found ourselves glancing at these rather than the Corvette's adjacent hybrids, probably because of the latter's relatively tight scales. Also, though it wasn't in our test ZX, Nissan's optional digital/hybrid display is even worse: Not only is it difficult to read; it's ugly.

What we really prefer is the ZX's standard instrumentation; large, legible, round gauges. Its only shortcoming is placement of the oil pressure/temperature and boost gauge up on the center console, though these are canted toward the driver to help matters. Below the main cluster is a diagnostic display, warning of

everything from lamp failures to door or hatch ajar, and also a pair of trip odometers (one for tank-to-tank and another for complete trip mileage?). Also, a pleasant-sounding lady in there somewhere warned us whenever a door was ajar. As a rather more useful feature, there's even a little warning light on the air conditioning control panel that signals low Freon level.

Down on the center console are the transmission's OD lockout control and the one for setting shock firmness. We used each of these actively in spirited driving, and came away wishing we could locate them less haphazardly. Put the OD lockout atop the shift lever, we thought; and while you're about it, convince Chevrolet to do the same with its control.

Moving to the rear of the redesigned ZX, we found useful luggage space that was more convenient than with the Vette. The latter's high, long liftover weighed against it; its two lockable compartments were appreciated, however. ⟫➜

it's just that the computer knows more about the powertrain's requirements than you do. It won't invoke OD until the engine reaches full operating temperature. So let the coolant get up to 185 degrees Fahrenheit and try again.

There's no reason for 1st OD, so the computer ignores this overkill. Indeed, 1st gear is good for 43 mph if you insist on revving to 5000 rpm and, in fact, if your 1st-2nd upshift comes at anything beyond 40 mph, 2500 rpm or half-throttle—any one of these suffices—then the computer figures you're intent on having some fun. It then gives you 2nd direct and stays in direct as long as you're in 2nd or 3rd: Upshift, downshift, light on the throttle, heavy on it; the computer doesn't want to upset your enthusiastic driving with any unexpected shifting.

We conjecture that Corvette folks put this enthusiast-motoring idea in the computer's head before the on/off switch got its U.S. clean bill of health. Now that we can disengage it so automatic upshifts into 2nd or 3rd OD won't hamper our fun, we'd be interested in trying a 4 + 3 that allowed them when we ease up on the throttle.

In any event, now try an easy upshift from 1st to 2nd. The computer gives you 2nd OD and, if you're a nostalgic sort,

you're reminded of what it must have been like driving one of those aero-engine Edwardian cars geared for three thumps per telly pole. For instance, a 1st-gear upshift at 2000 rpm and 17 mph gives you 2nd OD at 900 rpm. Thump, thump, thump. If you're not into Edwardian motoring, perhaps you'd best leave the OD disengaged in slow city traffic.

Then again, suppose you are a latent Edwardian. Another gentle upshift finds you at 35 mph in 3rd OD, with the engine turning a lazy 1250 rpm. A hole opens in the traffic and you'd like to fill it. Time for a downshift? Yes, but let the computer show its stuff: Punch the throttle (anything more than half) and there's an automatic downshift into 3rd direct. Engine revs jump from 1250 to around 1900, and you're off with what feels precisely like an automatic transmission's kickdown—as well it should, because the mechanisms involved are essentially identical. Once you fill that hole, you can upshift gently into top and the computer snags 4th OD automatically. You're going perhaps 45 mph by now, back in the Edwardian mode at 1250 rpm.

Get up to highway speeds now, say 60 mph. In 4th OD at this speed, engine revs are a leisurely 1650. And if you'd

care to switch the Vette's fuel-economy gauge to its instantaneous mode, you'll see around 26 mpg with a steady throttle foot (or cruise control) on a level road. Switch off the OD, the revs rise to 2450 in 4th direct and mpg drops to around 18. Humm. What can we learn from this?

One thing we did learn was that 4 + 3 fuel economy, even with all this wizardry, is little different from that with the automatic. We recorded 15.0 mpg, versus 15.5 for the car with the Turbo Hydra-matic, and that sounds like a wash.

Now, continue your highway trip in 4th OD and pretend you're driving a car with a conventional automatic transmission. Mash it, and the computer kicks down to 4th direct in exactly the same manner as a conventional automatic; 4th OD returns when you let off the throttle or (heaven forbid) should you be rash enough to reach 110 mph or so with foot to the wood.

It helps, of course, to understand all the nuances of the 4 + 3's shift strategy so you and it can become good friends. Get to know it and, like us, you may find yourself irritated occasionally when your conventional 5-speed refuses to grab a lower gear when you punch it.

—*Dennis Simanaitis*

PERFORMANCE

	Chevrolet Corvette	Nissan 300-ZX Turbo
Acceleration:		
Time to distance, sec:		
0–100 ft	3.1	3.2
0–500 ft	8.3	8.4
0–1320 ft (¼ mi)	15.6	15.7
Speed at end of ¼ mi, mph	88.5	86.0
Time to speed, sec		
0–30 mph	2.4	2.6
0–60 mph	7.1	7.4
0–80 mph	12.6	13.4
0–100 mph	21.4	23.0
Top speed, mph	136	133
Trip fuel economy, mpg	15.0	17.0
Brakes:		
Stopping distance, ft, from:		
60 mph	144	141
80 mph	250	249
Pedal effort for 0.5g stop, lb	20	18
Fade, % increase in effort,		
6 stops from 60 mph @ 0.5g	nil	nil
Overall brake rating	excellent	excellent
Handling:		
Lateral acceleration, g	0.880	0.795
Slalom speed, mph	63.2	62.8
Interior noise, dBA		
Idle in neutral	60	52
Maximum 1st gear	80	73
Constant 30 mph	67	66
50 mph	73	68
70 mph	77	73

Stand Back, Admire and Choose

ON ESTHETIC grounds, the Corvette did quite well for itself. We've come to admire its clean, well developed lines and, by and large, its fit and finish were very good. By contrast, we're not convinced the ZX has clearly profited from its reskinning. "It looks foreshortened," noted one staff member, "as though I'm seeing it through a slightly long lens." "Frumpy," was a more succinct second opinion. The ZX's paint and panels were well executed; there just seemed to be so many of the latter.

Within, the ZX continues this theme of busy detail, though the execution of all its shapes, shades and textures was well done. The Corvette's interior looked positively stark by contrast and a couple of us continue to think its flat plastic surfaces look excessively cheap in a car of this price.

When all the points were totaled, the 300-ZX emerged the winner, 630 to 538. The car amassed a goodly margin of points in those areas reflecting comfort and controls, though it surpassed the Vette in its performance subtotal as well. "So many things are hampered by the Vette's poor ride," summed up one

CUMULATIVE RATINGS—SUBJECTIVE EVALUATIONS

	Chevrolet Corvette	Nissan 300-ZX Turbo
Performance:		
Engine	32	**36**
Gearbox	28	**36**
Steering	**31**	28
Brakes	**35**	32
Ride	15	**35**
Handling	33	33
Body structure	19	**33**
Subtotals	193	**233**
Comfort/Controls:		
Driving position	30	**32**
Controls	31	**32**
Instrumentation	18	**32**
Outward vision	30	**32**
Quietness	16	**31**
Heat/vent/air conditioning	32	**34**
Ingress/egress	19	**31**
Seats	**30**	29
Luggage space & loading	16	**29**
Subtotals	222	**282**
Design/Styling:		
Exterior styling	**36**	24
Exterior finish	31	31
Interior styling	27	27
Interior finish	29	**33**
Subtotals	**123**	115
Totals	538	**630**
Staff members' preferences:		
Price-independent	5	**7**
Price-dependent	4	**8**

Four staff members' preferences, 1st choice, 2 points; 2nd choice, 1 point.

staff member, "though the 4+3 version appeals to me a lot more than the automatics I've driven."

"I agree," noted another staff member, "and I'll go one step further." He went so far as choosing the Corvette as his personal favorite in the cost-no-object mode, though his points margin in favor of the ZX was similar to those of his three colleagues. Clearly such an iconoclastic view called for amplification and, just as surely with our crowd, it followed: "The Corvette 4+3 is a boy racer, pure and simple," he said, "and, what's more, it does its boy-racer routine better than any other car I could

name. The ZX," he went on (we always seem to go on, don't we?), "is an extremely well executed sports/GT, but there are others of this genre I prefer." The other three drivers opted for the ZX regardless of who was paying and even our iconoclast admitted it offered more value, especially if comfortable, everyday sporting transportation is your goal.

So what began as a comparison of two apparently similar things concluded on a note of contrasting characters, each exemplary in its own way. Japan's answer to the Vette is alive and well; and so is America's answer to the Z-car.

Now we remember why we liked it so much

This is a case of visiting an old friend. This particular friend has been away for a while, and during the absence some changes have occurred—changes that, as friends, we wanted to check out. Checking out with an '84 Corvette, of course, dictates some special circumstances, including a rather circuitous route from the GM proving grounds in Mesa, Arizona, through the high mountains of central Arizona's Coconino Forest, and home to Los Angeles.

These high mountain roads are a driving junkie's nirvana. Banked corners, flat turns, uphills, downhills, speeds from 10 mph to what's-your-pleasure, all surrounded by the most impossible scenery and this wonderful, invisible, pure air. The Corvette on these roads is a sensory experience virtually impossible to duplicate, because both ingredients (the car and the road) are needed to make the magic work. The roads wouldn't be any fun in a VW Beetle, nor is the Vette very entertaining on a freeway—but put the two together and you'll never want it to stop, though of course it

finally must. Quite abruptly, the fun road ends in Quartzsite, Arizona. From there on, the mind-numbing I-10 drone to Los Angeles is punctuated only by watching Smokey pace back and forth, and fine-tuning the cruise control.

The rationale for all this fun was to see what a true production 4-speed Corvette was like (all our prior testing was with pre-production automatics) and evaluate the running production changes made by Chevrolet. New items are the overdrive lockout for the manual transmission and an engine oil cooler. Chevy has made the 16-in. tire/wheel package standard equipment, which eliminates the base wheel/tire, though as far as we were able to ascertain the base tire/wheel never existed anyway. Our test car was also fitted with the transparent roof panel, listed as an option since the introduction of the car but not available. The smoked acrylic panel itself employs some space-age high-tech, in the

PHOTOGRAPHY BY RICH COX, BOB D'OLIVO AND PAUL MARTINEZ

by Ron Grable

form of its abrasion-resistant coating. Developed for military fighter canopies, the ultra-thin layer can actually be scrubbed with a steel-wool pad without sustaining any scratches.

When the new Corvette was introduced back in March, the manual transmission option included a computer-controlled overdrive on the top three ratios. The overdrive decision was entirely the responsibility of the computer, and as is usually the case with computers, their thinking is a little labyrinthine. Driving was quickly reduced to waiting to see which gear the computer wanted, and most of the time it would select OD/direct when you least expected it—or needed it.

There was a reason for this computer tyranny, of course. When the original '84 Corvette was submitted for EPA certification, the schedules (conditions of road, load, and engine speed) were all completed in the automatic overdrive mode, and the mileage numbers thus generated were acceptably outside the "gas-guzzler" classification—with its per-vehicle fines and negative corporate image connotation. Inasmuch as the vehicle was certified in over-

'84 Corvette 4-Speed

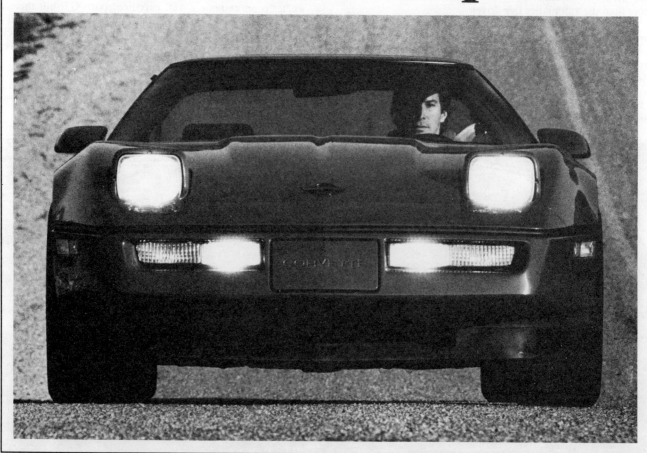

drive and was not certified otherwise, no "defeating" of the overdrive system was allowed.

Since the original certification, Chevrolet has been petitioning the EPA to accept a manual lockout of the automatic overdrive. The reasoning is that under conditions such as mountain driving (or any time the engine is needed to help decelerate the vehicle) the ability to lock out the overdrive would actually be a safety feature. Logic has finally prevailed, and EPA has given its permission for a "lockout" mode for the auto-overdrive, with no fuel mileage penalty.

Happy days are here again. It is a much more driveable car with the overdrive lockout function, and we find ourselves using the off position for most around-town driving, with the auto-OD mode selected as soon as a freeway on-ramp appears. Without the auto-OD, the transmission is a manual 4-speed in every sense of the word, except that at 114 mph in 4th gear, it forces overdrive (dropping the engine speed from 4700 rpm to 3200 rpm). The gear ratios are well fitted to the torque curve of the 350-cu-in. engine, but it is a

shock when overdrive is selected; the engine just falls on its face. The OD ratio is a staggering 0.67, and it seems like one engine revolution will take you just about to Topeka. To cite just one example, at 60 mph in the 1.0:1 4th gear, the engine is turning 2500 rpm (3.07:1 axle ratio). Punch the OD switch, and it falls all the way to 1700.

In the auto-OD mode, the transmission schedules are subtly different from the original, with some minor changes in the speeds at which the automatic shifts occur. With the new schedules, accelerating in 1st gear, when vehicle speed reaches 10 mph (at 18% throttle or less), the computer will interpret and remember the light throttle conditions as a light-load scenario, and when you upshift to 2nd, it will give you 2nd overdrive. If you continue the leisurely pace, the computer will maintain overdrive through the rest of the gears. If a contestant (the guy in the 911 is probably *still* talking to himself) or something else requiring haste happens by, a downshift can be forced by opening the throttle past 60%, after which the transmission will stay in direct drive with no further upshifts—until

4th is engaged and the other control parameters are met.

In 4th overdrive, if the car is manually downshifted (still in auto-OD) it will get 3rd overdrive, and on down to 2nd OD. The only way out of OD at this point is to load the engine above the parameters the computer needs to give you direct—then it will stay in direct until 4th is engaged and the other demand parameters are correct for overdrive.

If all this sounds intimidating and/or confusing—not to worry. It works very well in the real world, and after some short practice with the lockout switch, it's a "forget it." The only change we would like to see is a relocation of the switch itself. Reaching it in its present location (on the center console) requires lots of contortion, and the perfect location would seem to be the gear lever itself. Leaving it in the auto-OD mode around town increases the mileage, but it makes the engine labor at what feels like ultra-low rpm. We like it better in manual for city driving.

Roller-coasting around the mountain roads of Arizona, Mach .75 across the high-desert straights, or plodding around in L.A. commuter traffic, this is some sports car. It has some faults, but they are heavily outweighed by its virtues. The Vette tolerates freeways/stop-and-go/city streets, but it is in a holding mode for this kind of work, waiting to perform in the envelope for which it is intended. This is a car for having fun. Pure and simple. Take

another car freak with you and savor the look of amazement as he begins to understand the potential of this car.

This level of cornering performance does not come totally without cost, however, and the Corvette can be a harsh environment at times, on certain surfaces. For instance you definitely want to stay out of the far right lane on freeways that have seen lots of heavy 18-wheeler traffic. The Vette will jiggle your eyeballs on any surface the big rigs have roughed up. And if you are going out to see the top of the curve (on the graphic tachometer/speedo) in top gear on a narrow bumpy road, click your concentration up a couple notches. But so what? You pay attention when you land an F-15, right? And you don't land it on dirt runways. Like some multi-Mach fighter, this car is a thoroughbred and a specialist.

The new engine oil cooler does its job, and the maximum oil temperature we saw (after about 10 minutes at 135 mph plus) was 262° F—high but acceptable, considering the desert conditions. "Normal" usage only got the oil temperature in the 180-200° range. In previous experiences with Vettes, oil temperatures had always been the limiting factor in any sustained high-

speed running, with temperatures soaring above 300° F. This no longer seems to be a problem.

The transparent roof panel allowed too much of the Arizona sun into the car for our liking. We prefer the regular Vette roof, but the clear one does fit well and no excessive wind noise was noticed. In a heavy mountain shower, we did get a little water on the pants legs, so some additional attention is needed in the area of the windshield seal.

The '84 Corvette is as we remembered it: taut, responsive, predictable, and desirable. The running changes we've discussed here have addressed—and improved—a couple weak areas, areas that had been uniformly criticized. Does this mean Chevrolet is listening? We certainly would like to think so, because that bodes well for the future of this outstanding American representative in the GT arena. [MT]

ROAD TEST DATA

Chevrolet Corvette
☑ SPECIFICATIONS

GENERAL
Vehicle mfr.	Chevrolet Motor Div., General Motors Corp., Warren, Mich.
Body type	2-pass., 2-door coupe
Drive system	Front engine, rear drive
Base price	$23,360
Major options on test car	Power seats, power door locks, cruise control, leather seats, rear window defroster, Delco Bose Stereo system, Z-51 suspension package, engine oil cooler, transparent roof panel
Price as tested	$24,851 (est.)

ENGINE
Type	V-8, liquid cooled, cast iron block and heads
Displacement	5733 cc (350 cu in.)
Bore & stroke	101.6 x 88.4 mm (4.00 x 3.48 in.)
Compression ratio	9.0:1
Induction system	Rochester crossfire throttle body fuel injection
Valvetrain	OHV
Crankshaft	Cast iron, 5 main bearings
Max. engine speed	4500 rpm
Max. power (SAE net)	205 hp @ 4300 rpm
Max. torque (SAE net)	290 lb-ft @ 2800 rpm
Emission control	Oxygen sensor, EGR, 3-way catalyst
Recommended fuel	91 RON unleaded

DRIVETRAIN
Transmission		4-sp. man. w/electronic overdrive
Transmission ratios (1st)		2.88:1
	(2nd)	1.91:1 (1.28:1 O.D.)
	(3rd)	1.33:1 (0.89:1 O.D.)
	(4th)	1.0:1 (0.67:1 O.D.)
Axle ratio		3.31:1
Final drive ratio		2.21:1

CAPACITIES
Crankcase	3.8 L (4.0 qt)
Cooling system	13.7 L (14.5 qt)
Fuel tank	75.7 L (20.0 gal)
Luggage	507.0 L (17.9 cu ft)

SUSPENSION
Front	Independent, upper and lower A-arms, transverse plastic monoleaf spring, Bilstein gas-filled shocks
Rear	Independent, trailing arms, lateral struts, adjustable tie rods, transverse plastic spring, Bilstein gas-filled shocks, anti-roll bar

STEERING
Type	Rack and pinion, power assist
Ratio	13.0:1
Turns, lock to lock	2.0
Turning circle, curb to curb	40.1 ft

BRAKES
Front	11.5-in. vented discs, power assist
Rear	11.5-in. vented discs, power assist

WHEELS AND TIRES
Wheel size, f/r	16 x 8.5 in., 16 x 9.5 in.
Wheel type	Cast aluminum
Tire size	P255/50VR16
Tire mfr. & model	Goodyear Eagle VR50
Tire construction	Steel-belted radial

DIMENSIONS
Curb weight	1429 kg (3150 lb)
Weight distribution (%), f/r	51/49
Wheelbase	2438 mm (96.0 in.)
Overall length	4483 mm (176.5 in.)
Overall width	1803 mm (71.0 in.)
Overall height	1191 mm (46.9 in.)
Track, f/r	1514/1534 mm (59.6/60.4 in.)
Min. ground clearance	127 mm (5.0 in.)

CALCULATED DATA
Power to weight ratio	15.4 lb/hp
Top speed	144 mph
Drag coefficient	0.34

SKIDPAD
Lateral acceleration	0.88 g

FUEL ECONOMY (mpg)
EPA rating, city/hwy.	16/28
Test average	17.8

☑ TEST RESULTS

ACCELERATION
0-30 mph	2.80 sec
0-40 mph	4.44 sec
0-50 mph	5.80 sec
0-60 mph	7.58 sec
0-70 mph	10.17 sec
0-80 mph	13.03 sec
Standing quarter mile	15.88 sec/87.6 mph

SPEEDOMETER
Indicated	30	40	50	60
Actual	32	41	50	60

BRAKING
30-0 mph	33 ft
60-0 mph	127 ft

Chevrolet Corvette

King of the road, reborn.

• The white golf shirts that the Corvette guys handed out with a grin at Chevrolet's 1985 press preview say it all. Stenciled over the left breast are the Corvette crossed-flags insignia and the words "Life Begins at 150." Yes, that's *miles per,* and yes, for the first time in more than a decade, Chevy's plastic bi-seater will hit the magic one-five-oh mark. How sweet it is.

The Corvette engineering group has every right to crow about its latest victory over the laws of physics, but the message has meaning above and beyond speed. As far as we're concerned, 1985 is the year life begins for the new Corvette, period. Forget all the bad things you may know about this car; the slate is now wiped clean. The new model may not look any different, but by every measure it's a born-again automobile.

No one could be more happy about—or surprised by—this turn of events than your friendly road testers. We've flip-flopped on the Corvette more times than a politician switches positions on the issues. We heralded it as a breakthrough car after our initial proving-ground drives in early 1983, but after living with Corvettes in the harsh Midwestern road environment, we realized how badly we'd been duped. On anything but table-top-smooth pavement, the 1984 Corvette had a permanent mean streak. It squeaked and rattled, it quaked and shivered, it bucked and jostled like a Brahma in the chute. The handling was snaky, and the gearboxes were rough. We had hoped the new Corvette would be Chevrolet's answer to the Porsche 928. What we got was a car with an attitude problem.

But this is 1985, and it's a new ball game. When early tests indicated that the Corvette had changed its way of living, we tooled up a full-scale investigation similar to the one that had revealed the shocking truth about the 1984 Corvette. The major elements of this probe are as follows: a brace of pilot-line 1985 Corvettes, representing all the available suspensions and drivetrains; a 112.5-mile route through rural and suburban Michigan for back-to-back comparisons, buttressed by hundreds of miles of everyday use; our usual battery of track tests; and six *C/D* editors charged with bringing back the truth.

If you're wondering why we would lavish so much attention on a car that's already been under the microscope, you're underestimating the magnitude of the changes here. Though the tightly knit Corvette en-

gineering team is always loath to admit their car has *any* failings, the fact is that they've spent the past eighteen months worrying over just about every major system under the Corvette's taut skin.

Number one on the hit parade is the new L98 engine. For 1985, the Corvette's 5.7-liter V-8 is no longer strangled by an ineffi-

cient throttle-body fuel-injection system. In its place is the same basic port fuel-injection setup found on the Z28's optional LB9 five-liter V-8. The system, which includes a mass-airflow sensor, a generous intake plenum, elegant tuned intake runners, and computer control, makes the scenery under the clamshell hood as pretty as any-

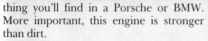

thing you'll find in a Porsche or BMW. More important, this engine is stronger than dirt.

Torque is the L98's claim to fame. The objective was to boost low-end punch to make the Corvette comfortable with significantly taller gearing. The strategy works well in helping the thirsty Vette scrape past the ever tighter gas-guzzler tax again, without hurting performance.

The numbers are impressive. Horsepower is up from 205 to 230 at 4000 rpm. Torque jumps from 290 pounds-feet to 330 at 3200 rpm. Even by the EPA's new, stricter rating system, which downgrades last year's city fuel-economy numbers by ten percent, the Corvette scores 16 mpg—not bad at all.

With more power available, the Corvette guys decided to shoot for a little magic. Says Corvette chief engineer Dave McLellan: "I told Jim [Ingle, a development engineer] to keep tweaking until he got 150." The result is that the 1985 Corvette sits a quarter-inch closer to the pavement. The changes improve aerodynamic penetration, lowering the Corvette's drag coefficient from an already admirable 0.34 to 0.33. The 150-mph goal is also the reason that a 3.07:1 final-drive ratio is now in the lineup (the standard axle is a taller 2.73). "The 3.07 is our top-speed axle," says McLellan. "That's all it's there for."

After the speed came the savvy. This year, both the base suspension and the Z51 racer package have been completely recalibrated to eliminate rudeness. Base cars now roll down the road on 26 percent softer front springs and 25 percent softer rear springs. The anti-sway bars have not been changed, but you can now buy Delco-Bilstein gas-pressure shock absorbers with the base suspension. Caster has been increased from three to four degrees on all cars to shore up straight-line stability. A larger master cylinder, a bigger power-brake booster, and different brake linings improve braking power and feel.

The effort expended on the all-out Z51 suspension is largely a result of Chevrolet's high hopes for the Corvette in the SCCA's Showroom Stock ranks. "The Z51 is our Showroom Stock GT car," says McLellan flatly. For that reason, the final tuning was carried out by Corvette development boss John Heinricy and his crew last winter at Firebird Raceway in Arizona. You can't get any racier than that.

For the 1985 Z51 package, the spring rates are down by sixteen percent in front and by 25 percent in the rear. All Z51s are fitted with new, larger anti-sway bars to keep total roll stiffness at 1984 levels. Delco-Bilstein shocks are now standard, and once again Z51s have quicker steering. The larger, 9.5-inch-wide wheels are now used all around rather than at the rear only.

To prepare the Z51 for the rigors of racing, it's also fitted with a heavy-duty cooling system, an oil cooler, and the 3.07:1 "top speed" final-drive ratio. "When we were done with the new Z51," says Heinricy, "it was one second per lap quicker than the 1984 setup at Firebird—with the same engine." Dropping in the more powerful 1985 drivetrain slashed another second off the lap time.

The gearboxes were next in line for fine tuning. This year's four-speed automatic benefits from new lockup-torque-converter programming to reduce the endless cycling that drove us crazy in last year's Corvette. The four-speed manual with computer-controlled overdrive has been improved in two ways. First, a neatly integrated overdrive button atop the shifter replaces the awkward console-mounted rocker switch. Second, the computer program that controls the thinking overdrive has been simplified to keep its interference at a minimum. Once again, you can lock out the overdrive entirely or use it at will on any of the three upper gears.

Then there are the dozens of small improvements. Recognizing that early 1984 Corvettes were rattletraps, the development group put Walt Banacki on the case full time to eliminate them. Banacki is the squeak-and-rattle exorcist who tamed the first downsized GM full-size cars, back in 1977. By the time he was done with the 1985 Corvette, 200 small structural changes had been proposed to cure everything from fender flutter to dash chirp. Chevrolet claims to have implemented 90 percent of Banacki's proposals already.

In the cabin, attention was paid to three areas. The graphics on the video-game dash were reworked for greater clarity. Optional leather covers were made available for the extra-cost, fully adjustable space-lounge sport seats. And the optional Delco-GM/Bose sound system was fully re-tuned to the interior acoustics.

The happy news is that every change is in the right direction. In fact, the new Vette is so good, it makes your heart soar. Our two test cars were a base-suspension version equipped with the automatic and a Z51 with the manual gearbox, both of them loaded. Within the first few miles, two things became, as Mr. Nixon used to say, perfectly clear: the new Corvette is tight and solid indeed, and we had strapped ourselves into a land rocket.

These cars virtually catapult off the line—especially the automatic, which rips to 60 mph in only 5.7 seconds and scorches the quarter-mile in 14.1 seconds at 97 mph. It's a full second quicker in both tests than last year's car. The manual is no slouch, either, with a 60-mph charge of six seconds flat and a quarter-mile of 14.4 seconds at 95 mph. That puts the automatic within a tick of the sensationally quick Porsche 911 Carrera; both cars are faster than the 928. And they just keep on going, all the way to an honest 150 mph.

In fact, the new Corvette makes great numbers in any direction. Roadholding is up at the 0.84-g mark for both versions, as high as we've ever seen for mass-produced cars. Braking from 70 mph is in the 182-to-185-foot range, some of the shortest stopping distances around. Our test cars even managed respectable gas mileage during our hard-charging test, the automatic delivering 16 mpg, the manual coming in at 17. All of these figures spot the new Vettes right there with the best Porsches and Ferraris—or whatever else you care to choose from the exotic ranks.

That's really no different from last year's story, though. What the numbers don't convey is how easily these cars drive fast—really fast—on any kind of road. No doubt about it, your mother could race around like a champ in a new Corvette.

We're referring here primarily to the base-suspension model we tested, with the optional Delco-Bilstein shocks. The Z51 is also radically improved, but it's still shaded toward the race-car end of the performance spectrum; it strikes most of us as a little too stiff, too quick-steering, and too nervous on beat-up two-lane pavement. The Z51 tuning does clearly pay off at the track (our slalom times showed it to be significantly faster than the base car), so we'd recommend it primarily for you hard-core enthusiasts who'll be doing Showroom Stock or Solo II events.

But the base-suspension model is the Corvette we wished for in the first place. It's so fast and so sure-footed that you'll find yourself calmly driving around at speeds that would have your eyes on sticks in most other cars. In terms of point A to point B on minimal expenditures of time and adrenaline, the Corvette may be the absolute top of the heap in America.

Best of all, the Corvette now does all this without ever hammering on you—something we can't say enough about. It's stable at warp speeds. The driving position is great, and the optional sport seats are nearly perfect (the base buckets are plenty good, too). Both transmissions work well, and far better than before. Indeed, this car's performance envelope is so far-reach-

ing, it's virtually the king of any road. And it makes you feel the same.

Oh, sure, it's got rough spots. The digital dash is still not as good as a top-flight analog setup. The manual shifter sounds trashy. It's work to get into and out of the driver's seat. The throttle response on the automatic car is way too sensitive around

COUNTERPOINT

• John Heinricy is the man of the hour, at least in my book. I met this Chevy engineer years ago at the X-car's introduction and knew at the time that he was capable of great things. For once, I was right: as project manager in the Corvette development department, Heinricy has systematically ground nearly all the rough edges off the controversial two-seater. Of course, he had plenty of support: from a chief engineer wise enough to let John have his way, from the small but effective group of road-racer development engineers who work with him, and from a Chevrolet division willing to spend a few million to make the Corvette better, immediately after spending many millions to make it merely new.

I'm glad to say that every penny was well invested. Like the 1984 model, this year's Corvette will perform miraculous roadholding feats, but now you can actually stand to live with the steering responses and ride motions that come as part of the deal. While I would never call this car plush, it's no longer a punishment chamber. The controversy is over, as far as I'm concerned: the new Corvette finally acts as good as it looks. I tip my editorial hat to the John Heinricys of the world. —*Don Sherman*

Dave McLellan's team has worked wonders on the 1985 Corvette. The punishing ride that made the 1984 car unacceptable to many drivers is now history. So are its hair-raising passing maneuvers, in which the car's path was so affected by bumps that it was rarely within a foot of where you wanted it. Even the symphony of squeaks and rattles that accompanied the car's progress is greatly subdued.

The Corvette boys have not only eliminated the car's weaknesses but increased its strengths as well. Power and performance are up to indisputably world-class levels. Both the automatic and the manual transmission perform with admirable smoothness and logic. And the handling is better than ever.

The Corvette is still burdened by its pinball-parlor instrument cluster, its poor chassis-body rigidity, and its irritating tendency to transform vertical bumps into lateral disturbances. But if you appreciate the sheer joy of a wheel-spinning start, a plastered-to-the-door-panel entrance ramp, or a blindingly sudden lane change, the Corvette is hard to beat. —*Csaba Csere*

I still wouldn't buy a plastic mastodon, but now there are more reasons than mere appearances to recommend the Vette to somebody who's just *got* to have one. And to anybody who leaped without more than a look, I say, dump yours and get thee into this new one. It's a very different car. Improvements? Oh, yes! Major improvements to handling and drivetrain, which, though still a bit shaky at times, demonstrate about ten times more coordination and willingness than in the past.

Year by year, just as if it were a German firm, Chevrolet is bettering its car. The difference is that the Germans start by turning out a supremely stout body and chassis, which are exactly the basics needed to create an unshakable impression of completeness and quality. Only then are the rest of the car's systems and features unified into the whole. Utterly solid structure is a basic that's still missing in the Corvette, and I don't yet feel it will be wonderfully, faithfully durable. But it's better than before, and, in telling you to leap right in, my conscience is clear. Make that reasonably clear. —*Larry Griffin*

Vehicle type: front-engine, rear-wheel-drive, 2-passenger, 3-door coupe

Estimated price as tested (Manual): $27,800

Estimated price as tested (Automatic): $27,500

Options on test car (Manual): Delco-GM/Bose sound system, transparent roof panel, leather sport seats, Delco-Bilstein shocks, cruise control, power driver's seat, power door locks, rear-window defogger, heavy-duty radiator, Z51 suspension.

Options on test car (Automatic): same as above minus Z51 suspension.

Sound system: Delco-GM/Bose AM/FM-stereo radio/cassette, 4 speakers, 25 watts per channel

ENGINE
Type .... V-8, iron block and heads
Bore x stroke .... 4.00 x 3.48 in, 101.6 x 88.4mm
Displacement .... 350 cu in, 5733cc
Compression ratio 9.0:1
Engine-control system........... GM/Chevrolet Computer Command Control
Emissions controls.....3-way catalytic converter, feedback fuel-air-ratio control, EGR, auxiliary air pump
Valve gear .... pushrods, hydraulic lifters
Power (SAE net) .... 230 bhp @ 4000 rpm
Torque (SAE net) .... 330 lbs-ft @ 3200 rpm
Redline .... 5500 rpm

DRIVETRAIN (Manual)
Transmission........... 4-speed with electronic overdrive
Final-drive ratio .... 3.07:1, limited slip

Gear	Ratio	Mph/1000 rpm	Max. test speed
I	2.88	8.5	47 mph (5500 rpm)
II	1.91	12.8	70 mph (5500 rpm)
II OD	1.28	19.0	105 mph (5500 rpm)
III	1.33	18.3	101 mph (5500 rpm)
III OD	0.89	27.4	137 mph (5000 rpm)
IV	1.00	24.4	122 mph (5000 rpm)
IV OD	0.67	36.4	150 mph (4100 rpm)

DRIVETRAIN (Automatic)
Transmission....... 4-speed automatic with lockup torque converter
Final-drive ratio .... 3.07:1, limited slip

Gear	Ratio	Mph/1000 rpm	Max. test speed
I	3.06	8.0	44 mph (5500 rpm)
II	1.63	15.0	83 mph (5500 rpm)
III	1.00	24.4	122 mph (5000 rpm)
IV	0.70	34.8	150 mph (4300 rpm)

DIMENSIONS AND CAPACITIES
Wheelbase .... 96.0 in
Track, F/R .... 59.6/60.4 in
Length .... 176.0 in
Width .... 71.0 in
Height .... 46.6 in
Frontal area.................................... 19.3 sq ft
Ground clearance................................... 5.0 in
Curb weight, manual/auto .... 3292/3257 lbs
Weight distribution, F/R (manual) 50.9/49.1%

town. The brakes still don't seem to have the endless high-speed reserves of Porsche binders. And we doubt whether the long-term quality of the Corvette body structure and trim pieces is up to the level of the German brands.

On the other hand, there's a lot to be said for a car that can run with the very best GTs in the world, in any contest or on any road, with the same kind of confidence and poise—and deliver it all for a fraction of the cost of the big-name brands. But of all the things we could say, the one that gives us the most pleasure is this: Ladies and gentlemen, the Chevrolet Corvette has finally arrived.

—*Rich Ceppos*

Fuel capacity . . . . 20.0 gal
Oil capacity . . . . 4.5 qt
Water capacity . . . . .14.6 qt

CHASSIS/BODY
Type . . . full-length frame integral with body-cage structure
Body material . . . . fiberglass-reinforced plastic

INTERIOR
SAE volume, front seat . . . . 49 cu ft
          trunk space . . . . 18 cu ft
Front seats . . . . bucket (6-way power driver's seat)
Recliner type . . . . infinitely adjustable
General comfort . . . . poor fair good **excellent**
Fore-and-aft support . . . . poor fair good **excellent**
Lateral support . . . . poor fair good **excellent**

SUSPENSION
F: . . .ind, unequal-length control arms, fiberglass-reinforced plastic leaf spring, anti-sway bar
R: . . . . ind; fixed-length half-shaft, 2 lateral links, and 2 trailing links per side; fiberglass-reinforced plastic leaf spring; anti-sway bar

STEERING
Type . . . . rack-and-pinion, power-assisted
Turns lock-to-lock 2.5 (Z51: 2.0)
Turning circle curb-to-curb . . . . 40.1 ft

BRAKES
F: . . . . 11.5 x 0.8-in vented disc, aluminum calipers
R: . . . . 11.5 x 0.8-in vented disc, aluminum calipers
Power assist . . . . vacuum

WHEELS AND TIRES
Wheel size . . . . 8.5 x 16 in (Z51: 9.5 x 16 in)
Wheel type . . . . cast aluminum
Tires . . . . Goodyear Eagle VR50, P255/50VR-16
Test inflation pressures, F/R . . . . 35/35 psi

CAR AND DRIVER TEST RESULTS

ACCELERATION (Manual) — Seconds
Zero to 30 mph 2.1
     40 mph 3.0
     50 mph 4.5
     60 mph 6.0
     70 mph 8.1
     80 mph 10.3
     90 mph 13.1
    100 mph 16.8
Top-gear passing time, 30–50 mph 5.2
               50–70 mph 5.0
Standing ¼-mile . . . . .14.4 sec @ 95 mph
Top speed . . . . .150 mph

ACCELERATION (Automatic) — Seconds
Zero to 30 mph 1.9
     40 mph 3.0
     50 mph 4.2
     60 mph 5.7
     70 mph 7.5
     80 mph 9.9
     90 mph 12.8
    100 mph 16.5
Top-gear passing time, 30–50 mph 3.1
               50–70 mph 4.1
Standing ¼-mile . . . . .14.1 sec @ 97 mph
Top speed . . . . .150 mph

HANDLING (Base Suspension)
Roadholding, 300-ft-dia skidpad . . . . 0.84 g
Understeer . . . . minimal **moderate** excessive
Maneuverability, 1000-ft slalom . . . . 62.5 mph

HANDLING (Z51)
Roadholding, 300-ft-dia skidpad . . . . 0.84 g

Understeer . . . . minimal **moderate** excessive
Maneuverability, 1000-ft slalom . . . . 64.5 mph

BRAKING (Base Suspension)
70–0 mph @ impending lockup . . . . 185 ft
Modulation . . . . poor fair **good** excellent
Fade . . . . **none** moderate heavy
Front-rear balance . . . . .poor **fair** good

BRAKING (Z51)
70–0 mph @ impending lockup . . . . 182 ft
Modulation . . . . poor fair **good** excellent
Fade . . . . **none** moderate heavy
Front-rear balance . . . . .poor **fair** good

COAST-DOWN MEASUREMENTS
Road horsepower @ 50 mph . . . . 14.5 hp
Friction and tire losses @ 50 mph . . . . 7.0 hp
Aerodynamic drag @ 50 mph . . . . 7.5 hp

FUEL ECONOMY (Manual)
EPA city driving . . . . **16 mpg**
EPA highway driving . . . . **22 mpg**
C/D observed fuel economy . . . . **17 mpg**

FUEL ECONOMY (Automatic)
EPA city driving . . . . **16 mpg**
EPA highway driving . . . . **23 mpg**
C/D observed fuel economy . . . . **16 mpg**

INTERIOR SOUND LEVEL (Manual)
Idle . . . . 61 dBA
Full-throttle acceleration . . . . 87 dBA
70-mph cruising . . . . 76 dBA
70-mph coasting . . . . 75 dBA

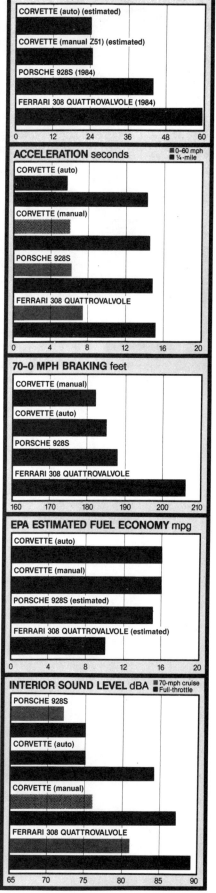

CORVETTE: BORN TO RUN?

The 1986 model of Chevrolet's most enduring sports car has at last arrived. We travelled to Europe to drive it

It is paradoxical, in a time when trade protectionism is still — just — regarded as a Bad Thing, that national construction regulations should make importing the cars of some countries so very awkward. Of course there are a host of other obstacles, particularly if you want to bring in an American car. Major difficulties are the strong dollar making the price too high, and, for the less experienced driver, the lack of any British market, meaning no right-hand drive and more difficulty than usual in obtaining spare parts.

Less vital are objections like the correct fuel not yet being easily available, to the detriment of your catalytic converter — what a shame — and the lamps, which do not conform to British ideas.

All of which is a pity, because if it is the 1986 model year Chevrolet Corvette that takes your fancy — as it certainly does ours — you will have to do a special deal with one of the four General Motors-appointed dealers here, or else trot over to GM Antwerp, as we did to carry out the first British test of this revised for '86 car.

Revised? Faithful *Autocar* readers will recall that we went to Belgium in 1984 to test the then new Corvette. That model was an automatic, but it still went superbly quickly, if spoiled by the unnecessarily stiff ride which made it difficult to drive fast over uneven country roads, and a nonsense of the claims for its cornering power. It was a curious error of design judgment, ruining an otherwise fascinating, highly un-American, high performance two-seater of unusually enterprising technical features and, in our opinion, marvellously clean good looks, in the massive American school.

Two main things have happened to the current Corvette since its February, 1983 birth. In place of the original twin throttle-body single-point system, the well known 'small block' 350 cubic inch (5733cc) V8 now has multi-point electronic fuel injection (with Bosch injectors and hot-wire flow sensing) which, together with a much better tuned-length separate tract inlet manifold, increases output from 198bhp at 4200rpm to 232 at 4100 (in Anglo-American James Watt horsepower — the metric figures are 201 to 235PS DIN). Torque is even more boosted, from 290 to 330lb ft; both occur at 2700rpm.

The other big improvement, of more importance, is the slight softening of the suspension, with the rates of the transverse single glass-fibre composite leaf springs at each end reduced from 148/219lb/in front/rear to 93/130. The hefty front (24mm dia) and rear (20mm) anti-roll bars are not changed, but Bilstein co-operated with Delco in producing the gas dampers. (Delco also got together with loud speaker manufacturer Bose to produce the sophisticated ambionic four-speaker radio-cassette system found in this version of the car.) The already effective all-disc brakes with their Girlock aluminium/alloy calipers now have Bosch-developed anti-lock control as standard, with Mercedes-style three-channel wheel speed sensing, separately in each wheel, and jointly on the back.

Outside, the sleekly fat body has a bigger front air dam and slightly lowered ride height to bring the already good 0.34 drag coefficient (measured in GM's huge tunnel at Warren, Michigan) down to a claimed 0.323 — that seems to be without the roof stop lamp fitted to the test car.

The car we tried this time was the four-speed manual 'box version, which has always had the unusual feature of an electrically switched-in 0.67-to-1 overdrive, which if you set it (by pressing a switch formed in the top of the gear lever) comes in automatically in any of the upper three gears whenever you relax the right foot. It disengages if you 'kick-down' the accelerator, and the ratios are such that when hitched to fourth gear it is effectively a near-enough perfect top for this Chevrolet to realise the absolute maximum speed for its peak power delivery — 151mph as an average of maximum speed runs in opposite directions, which the car does with relatively superb ease and certainly immaculate stability.

We detected no signs of front-end lift or wander — the Corvette just ran, roaring gloriously on and on, straight as a die, to an accompaniment of bangs like rapid rifle fire from the expansion joints in the motorway concrete.

As the overdrive kicks out whenever you use the power even a little, you can't measure the performance in overdrive except above its maximum kick-down speed in fourth, 78mph. Accelerate flat-out in direct fourth with the overdrive set, and the 'box doesn't engage the overdrive until a true 104mph (4250rpm, an ideal change speed in view of the 4100 power peak). As a way of achieving a five-speed gearbox if you don't want to make one, using an overdrive was a ploy used extensively by British manufacturers 10 to 20 years ago.

The Corvette overdrive resurrects an old objection to such devices — their jerky engagement and disengagement, which is particularly noticeable here. It wouldn't be so noticeable if GM only allowed the epicyclic to come in on fourth gear, which is all that is needed. As it is, if you have left it set, and dare driving, say, around a motorway entry turn, you can all too easily find the 'box hunting abruptly in and out of overdrive second or third.

As the figures show, this Corvette goes. The engine is a delight, pulling hard from 1000rpm and certainly not objecting to working from below 10mph in fourth, at 400rpm, on lead-free fuel. Its full stride is ▶

Digital display *instrumentation is comprehensive and clear*

Flat load *area conceals cleverly designed luggage lockers*

Small-block V8 *now has multi-point electronic injection*

Rear lights *retain traditional round shape. Filler flap is in centre*

TEST UPDATE

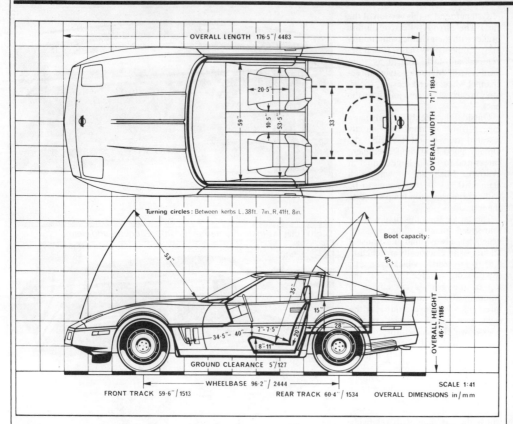

OVERALL LENGTH 176·5"/4483

OVERALL WIDTH 71"/1804

Turning circles: Between kerbs L, 38ft. 7in, R, 41ft. 8in.

Boot capacity:

GROUND CLEARANCE 5"/127

WHEELBASE 96·2"/2444

FRONT TRACK 59·6"/1513

REAR TRACK 60·4"/1534

OVERALL HEIGHT 46·7"/1186

SCALE 1:41

OVERALL DIMENSIONS in/mm

MODEL

CHEVROLET CORVETTE

PRODUCED BY:
Chevrolet Motor Division, General Motors Corporation, Bowling Green, Kentucky, USA

Not officially available in the UK

SPECIFICATION

ENGINE
Longways front, rear-wheel drive. Head/block cast iron/cast iron. 8 cylinders in 90deg V, bored block, 5 main bearings. Water cooled, electric fan.
Bore 101.6mm (4in), **stroke** 88.4mm (3.48in), **capacity** 5733cc (350 cu in).
Valve gear ohv, 2 valves per cylinder, hydraulic tappets, chain camshaft drive. **Compression ratio** 9 to 1. Electronic mapped ignition, electronic multi-port injection.
Max power 235bhp (PS-DIN) (173kW ISO) at 4100rpm. **Max torque** 330lb ft at 2700rpm.

TRANSMISSION
4-speed manual with automatic final-drive-mounted overdrive on 2nd, 3rd and top, clutch 10.75in dia.

Gear	Ratio	mph/1000rpm
OD Top	0.68	35.34
4th	1.00	24.37
3rd	1.34	18.20
2nd	1.91	12.77
1st	2.88	8.46

Final drive: Hypoid bevel (Posi-traction limited slip diff), Ratio 3.07.

SUSPENSION
Front, independent, glassfibre transverse leaf spring, wishbones, telescopic dampers, anti-roll bar.
Rear, independent, glassfibre transverse leaf spring, fixed length drive shafts, wishbone geometry links, telescopic dampers, anti-roll bar.

STEERING
Rack and pinion, hydraulic power assistance. Steering wheel diameter 14.5in, 2.45 turns lock to lock.

BRAKES
Dual circuits, anti-lock system, split front/rear. **Front** 11.5in (292mm) dia ventilated discs. **Rear** 11.5in (292mm) dia ventilated discs. Vacuum servo. Handbrake, left-hand lever acting on rear discs.

WHEELS
Aluminium alloy, 9.5in rims. Radial tyres (Goodyear Eagle on test car), size P255/50VR16, pressures F35 R35 psi (normal driving).

EQUIPMENT
Battery 12V, 50Ah. Alternator 97A. Headlamps 110/120W. Reversing lamp standard. 25 electric fuses. 2-speed, plus intermittent screen wipers. Electric screen washer. Air blending automatic interior heater; air conditioning standard. PVC seats, plastic foam headlining. Carpet with heel mat floor covering.

PERFORMANCE

MAXIMUM SPEEDS

Gear		mph	km/h	rpm
OD Top	(Mean)	151	243	4200
	(Best)	152	245	4250
4th	(Mean)	130	209	5350
	(Best)	132	212	5400
3rd		100	161	5500
2nd		70	113	5500
1st		47	76	5500

ACCELERATION FROM REST

True mph	Time (sec)	Speedo mph
30	2.1	31
40	3.1	41
50	4.6	51
60	6.0	61
70	8.4	71
80	10.4	81
90	13.0	92
100	16.5	101
110	19.8	111
120	24.6	121
130	32.0	132
140	41.5	141
150	62.2	151

Standing ¼-mile: 14.8sec, 95mph
Standing km: 26.9sec, 124mph

IN EACH GEAR

mph	OD Top	4th	3rd	2nd
10-30	—	—	6.2	4.3	2.7
20-40	—	5.1	3.8	2.5
30-50	—	4.9	3.6	2.3
40-60	—	4.8	3.4	2.6
50-70	—	4.8	3.4	—
60-80	—	4.6	3.8	—
70-90	—	4.8	4.9	—
80-100	9.1	5.5	—	—
90-110	9.5	6.6	—	—
100-120	10.6	8.2	—	—
110-130	13.3	10.4	—	—
120-140	17.2	—	—	—

CONSUMPTION

FUEL
Overall mpg: 17.6 (16.0 litres/100km) 3.87mpl
Autocar constant speed fuel consumption measuring equipment incompatible with fuel injection.
Autocar formula: Hard 15.8mpg
Driving   Average 19.4mpg
and conditions   Gentle 22.9mpg
Grade of fuel: lead-free, 2-star (76 RM)
Fuel tank: 16.7 Imp galls (76 litres)
Mileage recorder: accurate
Oil: (SAE 10W/30) negligible

BRAKING

Fade (from 95mph in neutral)
Pedal load for 0.5g stops in lb

start/end			start/end
1 20-20		6	40-50
2 20-25		7	40-40
3 25-40		8	40-60
4 30-45		9	45-50
5 40-50		10	45-50

Response (from 30mph in neutral)

Load	g	Distance
10lb	0.30	100ft
20lb	0.58	52ft
30lb	0.74	41ft
40lb	1.00	30ft
Handbrake	0.20	151ft

Max gradient: 1 in 4
CLUTCH Pedal 39lb; Travel 7in

WEIGHT

Kerb 28.3cwt/3173lb/1439kg
(Distribution F/R, 51.3/48.7)
Test 31.7cwt/3552lb/1611kg

COSTS

Car not on sale in UK

SERVICE & PARTS
Not available

WARRANTY
12 months/unlimited mileage

EQUIPMENT

Voltmeter	●
Automatic	○
Cruise control	○
Consumption gauge	●
Electronic ignition	●
Overdrive	○
Limited slip differential	●
Power steering	●
Rev counter	●
Steering wheel rake adjustment	●
Steering wheel reach adjustment	●
Headrests	●
Power seats	○
Height adjustment	○
Lumbar adjustment	○
Seat back recline	●
Door mirror remote control RH/LH	●
Electric windows	●
Heated rear window	●
Interior adjustable headlamps	N/A
Sunroof	●
Tinted glass	●
Headlamp wash/wipe	N/A
Alloy wheels	●
ABS brakes	●
Low profile tyres	●
Tyre size	255/50VR16
Central locking	●
Cigar lighter	●
Clock	●
Fog lamps	●
Internal boot release	●
Locking fuel cap	○
Metallic paint	○
Radio/cassette	○
Speakers	○
Aerial	○

● Standard ○ Optional at extra cost
N/A Not applicable † Part of option package DO Dealer option

TEST CONDITIONS

Wind:	0-5mph
Temperature:	5deg C (41deg F)
Barometer:	29.7in Hg (1010mbar)
Humidity:	85per cent
Surface:	dry asphalt and concrete
Test distance:	895miles

◄from 1700rpm, and stays so all the way to over 5000rpm, well beyond the power peak. There is no rev limiter, so you have to take care not to go beyond the red sector of the bar graph rev counter, which its digital display says begins at 5500rpm.

On first acquaintance, the accelerator linkage is a bit too responsive off the stop, so that you tend to blip unintentionally. The cruise control though, is wonderfully gentle when restoring speed after a pause, backing off perfectly as the car nears the pre-set rate again.

In spite of the standard-equipment limited slip differential, the best standing starts are a matter for restraint, as it is too easy with such power to spin the back wheels. About

3500rpm we found best; the clutch dropped in, then the throttle feathered until the big Goodyears bite to end two parallel black lines at the same instant.

The other limit on how well you can accelerate is the gearchange. It is in most respects very fine, with a dominantly machine-like feel, great precision in its heavy-ish, narrow-gated movement, and, with 3300 miles on its mileometer at any rate, totally unbeatable synchromesh. This last distinction is a good thing from most points of view, except when you are trying to really hurry the change, when no matter how hard you pull or push the lever, it will not be hustled.

Gearchange reluctance aside,

there is nothing to criticise in the '86 Corvette's performance; it is excellent, getting close to the acceleration figures we have recorded for most manual-gearbox European high performance cars, if not super-cars. What about those springing changes?

The test car was the Z51 Corvette sports, with spring rates stiffer than standard. Comparison with the original 1984 car would be unfair because the Z51 springing — 111lb psi front, 174 rear — is much softer than the 193/262 rate on the '84 car. But the Z51 is still remarkably stiff by any ride standards, failing to absorb bumps in a way that would be uncomfortable but for the effective seating. There is little roll. Steering (2½ turns lock to lock for a 40.5ft turning circle), is high geared, invoking fears of bump-steer sensitivity found on the earlier car.

Experience teaches you that the new Corvette is not like this; its superb high speed straight stability is mirrored in its stability at all other speeds, and in its very good road manners. Of course, with such power, you have to beware of using too much at the wrong moment, and converting the normal understeer into a tail slide, especially in the wet. But the car does nothing it shouldn't and although the near-uniformly high standard of European road surfaces is not a demanding test, the modifications make the 251 tolerable and the standard car probably reasonable. We shall have to wait to see.

It certainly hangs on in a smooth

bend marvellously, although high frequency bumps can make it patter outwards momentarily.

The anti-lock brakes work well in preserving stability and steering, if they take a little, as usual, from ultimate stopping ability — which for most drivers is of less importance than allowing them to preserve steering control.

Inside one finds a good driving position for up to 6ft pilots, but not so generous passenger legroom. The optional power seats fitted to the test car will enable every shape and size of driver to find just the right position. Even the lumbar support is well catered for in the form of three horizontal air bags which can be individually inflated or deflated to mould the seat to suit anyone. The very comprehensive digital instruments provide a full range of desirable information, while there is an impressive view forward.

The headband-like B-post is too broad for the best vision all round, but once you have overcome the stiffness of its mounting, the detachable roof panel (which fits neatly under the all-glass rear hatch) lifts off to give near-traditional sports car openness.

The '86 Corvette is still surprisingly unrefined, but who cares in what is one of the most satisfying high performing big sports cars now available? In the specification tested, it costs around 35,000 dollars, or £32,000 from one of the four GM dealers who can help.■

Lift-off *targa roof panel is stowed neatly under glass hatch*

Too much *power at the wrong moment will cause oversteer, but high-speed stability is excellent. It hangs on in smooth bends well, too*

'86½ Corvette Roadster

America's plastic fantastic topless tourer is back!

by Gary Witzenburg

PHOTOGRAPHY BY LYNNE MCCREADY AND BOB D'OLIVO

In the fall of 1975, not quite a year after he had replaced the legend named Zora Arkus-Duntov as Chevrolet's Corvette chief engineer, Dave McLellan was enjoying a well-deserved vacation with his wife, Glenda.

They spent several days cruising through and around California's gorgeous Yosemite National Park. In (what else?) a '75 Corvette. A convertible. With the top down.

"It was cold," he recalls, "and we were huddled close to the windshield with the heater on. But the three-dimensional scenery was so spectacular, *no way* were we going to put the top up and miss anything."

GM discontinued the Corvette convertible after 1975, but McLellan has nurtured memories of that trip ever since. And exactly 10 years later, he was able to relive the experience—with a small group of auto journalists along for the ride. The occasion was a special sneak preview of the first factory soft-top Corvette in slightly more than a decade.

Eight cars—four prototype '86½ ragtops, two '86 coupes (one standard, one Z51), a Mercedes 380SL, and a Porsche 911 Cabriolet (for comparison)—made up our entourage, each one equipped with a Corvette engineer.

We motored south on California 41 to Oakhurst, west on 49 to Mariposa, north on 140 through El Portal and into the park, stopping every so often to stretch our legs, change cars, and gaze at the scenery. The weather was bright, beautiful, and unseasonably warm. And the Corvette convertibles were near-perfect.

Even at extra-legal speeds, there's a lot less buffeting than in the coupe with its targa panel out. You do have to speak up, but conversation on the fly is no problem.

As intended, the roadster's handling is midway between the standard coupe's and the ultra-slick Z51's, yet its ride is comfortably supple. Structural stiffness—the lack of body shake over road irregularities, for example—is actually *better* than the coupe's.

The roadster transformation is a brilliant piece of engineering, especially considering that the new-generation Vette was not designed with toplessness in mind.

According the McLellan, it was less than two years ago when Heinz Prechter of ASC, Inc. (formerly American Sunroof Corporation) showed him an '84-based concept car. The decision to go ahead with the program came the following August, and rough prototypes soon were shuttling around the GM Proving Grounds. "Pilot-line" cars from production tooling were going together by the following October, and full production examples should be rolling off the line by the time you read this.

Unmodified Corvette roadsters will pace the 1986 Indy 500 (perhaps the first time Indy Pace Cars have needed no performance or handling "tuning"), and the first 6000 built will be Pace Car replicas, available sometime in April. After that, says McLellan, roadster production *could* continue at a 50% rate (if demand is that high), but most likely will be about 15% of the total '86 build.

Unlike other GM/ASC convertibles (Cavalier, Sunbird, and the recently discontinued Eldorado and Riviera), drop-top Vettes will be assembled right in the Bowling Green, Kentucky, plant rather than in a separate facility. ASC is responsible for the convertible top and framework, Chevrolet for the rest of the car.

'86½ Corvette Roadster

Structural reinforcements are extensive: The so-called "Wonderbar" between the frame rails, forward of the engine, is thicker. Beefier K-braces connect the frame rails to the under-engine crossmember. The front torque box, the steering column, and its mounting hardware all are stiffened. New conical, spring-loaded wedge pins strengthen the joints across the doors, while added X-braces connect the door hinge pillars to the opposite rear torque boxes. A double-panel seatback riser and an extra bar across the top of the rear torque box add cross-car stiffness, and there are even anti-shake restrictors in the power steering lines.

To compensate for this added weight, the top mechanism frame is aluminum, and roadsters will be first to get the new aluminum heads (with larger intake ports and a higher 9.5:1 compression ratio), which didn't quite make '86 production start-up last summer. Ride height is raised 0.4-in. to maintain ground clearance under the X-braces, while pressure in the giant (P255/50VR16) Goodyear Gatorbacks is dropped from 35 to 30 psi to improve their bump-eating abilities. Despite all this, the Corvette's outstanding roadholding is maintained, partly due to new-design Delco deflected-disc shocks and the Z51's 9.5-in. wheels.

The handsome convertible top stacks neatly beneath a hinged fiberglass cover in Corvette roadster tradition. Door-mounted switches (the same ones that pop open the coupe's rear hatch) operate solenoids to release the cover and the top mechanism's rear pins. Luggage room and access behind the seats is reduced, es-

> **Only those who've experienced one could know how absolutely, terribly, frighteningly seductive this new Corvette convertible really is**

pecially with the top stowed, but roadster folks are light travelers anyway. An optional removable hardtop will be offered later in the year.

Regular readers already know about the '86 Corvette's standard Bosch ABS II anti-lock brakes, its state-of-the-art Vehicle Anti-Theft System (VATS) with electrical codes built into the keys, and the glare-reducing new tilt of its Star Wars instrument cluster (*MT*, Oct. '85). They know its 230-horse port-injected 5.7-liter V-8, driving through either a 4-speed overdrive automatic or a 4-speed manual with electric overdrive in the top three gears, will propel a

Corvette coupe to 60 mph in a bit over 6 sec and a top speed well over 150 mph. Also that the less aerodynamic roadster should be good for "only" 140 or so.

But only those who've experienced one could know how absolutely, terribly, frighteningly seductive this new Corvette convertible really is. Next to it, the coveted Mercedes 380 ($44,000)

> **Luggage room is reduced, but roadster folks are light travelers anyway**

and Porsche 911 ($37,000) roadsters are overrated antiques.

No car is perfect, and the Corvette still needs more interior storage, real instruments (dials with pointers) for real drivers, and a less agricultural manual shift linkage. Still, it's probably already the world's best all-around sports car, and the reincarnated roadster version (at about $32,000) is easily the finest-driving open car money can buy.

After one long day of top-down touring amid Yosemite's breathtaking vistas, there wasn't one case among us who didn't desperately want one. [MT]

Chevrolet Corvette Convertible

Tod and Buz, your car is ready.

• The editorial "we" has shuttled between enchantment and annoyance so many times on the Corvette since its 1984 redesign that our tests read like soap-opera scripts. Is this the most advanced production car on the planet, as we once asserted, or an aluminum-and-fiberglass reincarnation of Judas Iscariot, as we later intimated? Stay tuned for the next thrilling episode as "we" neatly dodge the issue by saying, "Boy, it's sure a lot better than it was last year."

There should be no arguing over this latest assessment, for two reasons. For 1986, after a ten-year absence, a convertible version will once again be available. If you like convertibles, *hallelujah!* If you don't, the coupe continues as before.

The second reason to rejoice is the Bosch-derived anti-lock brake system, which is now standard on both body styles. The stopping distance from 70 mph is only 164 feet, the second shortest we've ever measured for a production car.

We'll come back to this headline stuff after a rundown of the news. Starting in February or March, both the convertible and the coupe will have aluminum cylinder heads as standard equipment. Although this change was originally intended for the start of the 1986 model run, a few design details had to be revised at the last moment, resulting in a delay. The heads do more than just save 40 pounds per car, though this is no small thing in itself. They also contribute to engine efficiency, thanks to the spark plugs' being more centrally located in the combustion chambers and to larger intake ports. And the compression ratio has been raised half a point, to

9.5:1—a typical change in the transition from iron to aluminum heads because of the faster heat transfer of aluminum.

Professional car thieves should have special interest in VATS, the new Vehicle Anti-Theft System, which is also standard equipment. Everyone will notice that the new ignition key has a black pellet inserted in the top of the blade just after the grooves and notches fade out. Anyone who tries to start a new Corvette without the right pellet in his key will notice a lot of cranking but not much starting. This pellet is the resistance module—Chevrolet has fifteen to choose from—and the ignition switch reads it along with the normal grooves and notches. If the key reader doesn't like the proffered pellet, it tells the electronic control module to deactivate certain parts of the fuel system (thieves

read this magazine too, so the less said about which parts, the better) for about two minutes. Therefore, a thief determined to use a key instead of a tow truck might have to shuffle little black pellets for as much as a half-hour before finding the right one. And the ordinary thief, Chevrolet says, thinks anything longer than ten minutes is working overtime. So there's a reasonable chance he'll ignore your Corvette, go on down the street, and pick out a nice Porsche instead.

Said thief will be missing out on a few other 1986-model changes. An upshift idiot light sits in the upper left corner of the tachometer. The whole instrument cluster has been slightly reangled to reduce glare. And a center-mounted brake light has been incorporated—at the top of the rear window on the coupe, at the top of the taillight panel on the convertible.

So much for details. Now back to the headlines. The convertible, clearly a nice piece of work, is a joint venture between Chevrolet and ASC, and it entailed far more than just peeling the top off of the coupe. The car's frame is considerably revised, in part by adding stiffness (including an X-brace under the cockpit floor), in part by reengineering sections of the original structure. The result is a convertible un-

commonly free of creaks and groans, particularly when you consider its stiff suspension. The few aftershocks you feel in the structure when you've passed over a bump are of very high frequency—by itself, a good indication of stiffness—and they damp out quickly. Certain trim pieces quiver and rustle for a longer time, but they do that in the coupe, too.

Our subjective conclusions about chassis stiffness are confirmed by Corvette engineers, who say that the convertible is not as rigid as the coupe when the latter's roof panel is in place, but it's better than the coupe with the panel removed. (This conclusion may soon have to be revised, though, because the engineers are considering adding the convertible's reinforcement package to the coupe.)

The convertible's roof, and its system of stowing, continue very much in the Cor-

Bigfoot, Thumper, and Puff

Driving the latest crystal-ball Corvettes.

• Corvette chief engineer Dave McLellan and his dedicated team are determined that the fast-paced development their car has enjoyed in its first three years will continue into the foreseeable future. Several clues to the Corvette's continuing evolution are revealed in a bevy of experimental cars that we sampled during a recent visit to GM's proving grounds in Milford, Michigan.

The first experimental Corvette we drove was named Bigfoot in honor of its wide racing tires, which are mounted on three-piece alloy wheels and covered with fender flares. To push its considerable traction to the limit, Bigfoot also has 400 hp under its hood. Bigfoot's role is to provide experience with suspension calibrations suitable for wider, stickier tires than Corvettes have today—perhaps 275/40R-17s. A brief drive demonstrated Bigfoot's excellent steering response and surprisingly pleasant ride.

Another experimental Corvette, called Thumper, has a Ryan Falconer–built, NASCAR-spec V-8 that produces about 600 hp. Its tremendous speed potential will be used to test the braking power and fade resistance of the thirteen-inch-diameter brake rotors and the two-piston calipers that are scheduled for 1988.

These brakes are also being evaluated

on some of the fourteen Puff the Magic Dragon prototypes. These Corvettes are fitted with twin-turbocharged and intercooled versions of the standard small-block V-8, yielding from 350 to 600 hp. McLellan and crew are using the Puff cars to explore turbocharging as a route to future power increases; in 400-hp form, the engine can push the Corvette to 180 mph, yet it is extremely tractable. Unfortunately, Chevrolet management has concluded that turbocharging the pushrod V-8 would have little technical or marketing appeal, so this approach will not see production. Chevy is, however, collaborating with Callaway Turbosystems, an aftermarket tuning outfit that plans to offer an emissions-legal twin-turbo package for those who don't want to wait for the final solution.

Increased power is clearly in the cards, and the Corvette engineers are working on a traction-control system to help put it to the pavement. Their system works in conjunction with the sensors and the computer of the anti-lock braking system to detect and limit wheelspin by selectively applying the rear brakes and reducing the engine's output. A brief drive in one of the traction-control cars showed impressive stability during full-throttle maneuvers on slick pavement. Different

Bigfoot is named for its wide, sticky tires.

control calibrations to suit a wide range of traction conditions are currently under development for a possible 1989 introduction.

Active suspension is also in the works. A concept car with such a system will be unveiled at the upcoming Chicago Auto Show, but it's only a teaser. A more serious effort is currently under way within the Chevrolet-Pontiac-Canada chassis-design group; it involves participation by Lotus in England, at least two Corvettes,

vette tradition. Two toggles release the folding top from the windshield header. Unlatching two tapered pins below the rear window releases the rear attachment. Then you lift the rear of the roof to allow the rear-hinged deck panel to swing open. In effect, the trunk then swallows the top, leaving no trace of it once the deck panel is returned to its place and latched. (There is still room in the trunk for a good-sized suitcase under the folded top.)

Except for four electric latches at the rear (two to release the top and two to allow the deck panel to open), all of the folding and swinging are accomplished manually, but the efforts are hardly worth mentioning. Getting out of the cockpit is the hardest part.

Back on the road, you'll find a top-down Corvette to be a mighty hospitable carriage. When there's no crosswind, air flows

smoothly around the occupants' heads, with no buffeting of their ears and with only modest tousling of their coiffures. New for 1986, on both the convertible and the coupe, are plastic fairings between the windshield pillars and the side mirrors; they do much to smooth out the airflow across the window openings. They are hardly things of beauty when viewed from the cockpit—you see inside them, which is rather like looking under a fender—but at least they are functionally elegant.

The swept-back form of the windshield provides a pocket of still air just behind the glass, but the gradient of air speed rises quickly as you measure back from the visors. By the time you reach the headrests there is a stiff breeze, but the flow is smooth rather than turbulent and therefore is not unpleasant.

The convertible's only serious annoyance exists only when the top is up: the rear quarters are so wide that they block the view to the corners. Visibility is so bad that you have to approach crossroads perpendicularly, no matter what angle the intersection, just so you can get a decent view of oncoming traffic.

Corvette engineers say there is no weight difference between the coupe and the convertible. Maybe that shouldn't be a

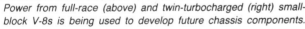

Power from full-race (above) and twin-turbocharged (right) small-block V-8s is being used to develop future chassis components.

PHOTOGRAPHY: AARON KILEY

and several other GM models. Active suspension is not yet scheduled for production, but the Corvette's reputation for technical leadership and its high price make it a logical candidate for the new system when it is ready.

All of these developments suggest that there is a super Corvette on the way. Although the twin-turbo engine has been rejected, massive power increases have not. It appears that Chevrolet will join forces with Lotus to produce a version of the V-8 that was unveiled in the 1984 Etna show car. With four cams, 32 valves, and five to six liters of displacement, this engine could easily produce 400 hp. To harness this power and still produce ac-

ceptable fuel economy, the Lotus-Chevrolet engine would be coupled to a proposed six-speed manual gearbox governed by a computer-regulated shift pattern. All in all, the combination of a 32-valve engine, an improved manual transmission, seventeen-inch tires, big brakes, and traction control makes perfect sense to us.

The Corvette of Chevy's dreams would not replace the current base model but might instead be offered as a king-of-the-hill version, with distinctive bodywork and a premium price tag. Although it might account for only a small fraction of total sales, such a car would indisputably establish the Corvette as the world's

fastest sports car—and that would please Chevrolet management very much.

Gradually, these various technological upgrades would spread through the rest of the line, along with further weight reductions, increased chassis stiffness, and a redesigned electronic instrument cluster. Such improvements should hold the Corvette in good stead until it's replaced by an all-new design in the early 1990s.

New concepts are now under consideration for the next-generation model; in fact, preliminary drafting is already under way at Hawtal Whiting Design and Engineering in England. A full report on those plans will follow as soon as our moles hit pay dirt. —*Csaba Csere*

surprise, because the huge glass terrarium on the back of the coupe could have been traded for a lot of steel reinforcements. It could also have been traded for a small glass window in the back of the convertible top, but Chevrolet took the easy way out by using plastic film—the kind that gets foggy in a few years. Our test car weighed 3266 pounds, within a few pounds of previous coupes with similar options. In any case, we see no reason to disagree with the engineers: with all the additions and deletions taken together, the '86 model, coupe or convertible, weighs virtually the same as the '85.

Radical surgery of the type that produces a convertible usually has a negative effect on ride quality. The engineers went to work to avoid any such deterioration, and the result is that the convertible has its own package of springs, bars, and shocks. The convertible's front spring rate is 310 pounds per inch, compared with 295 for the coupe. Both have 228-pound-per-inch springs in back and 26mm tubular front anti-roll bars. The convertible's 19mm rear bar, however, is smaller than the coupe's, which is 20mm. (In comparison, the coupe's Z51 handling option has 380-pound-per-inch springs in front, 330 in back, a 30mm solid front anti-roll bar and a 22mm solid rear bar.) Shock-absorber calibration is different for each model.

The convertible also departs from GM's usual 35-psi recommendation for tire pressure: its placard calls for 30 psi. This is purely a ride consideration. Corvette engi-

neers admit that nothing bad will happen to the coupe owner with ride complaints if he deflates accordingly, though they can't officially advise around the official recommendation, if you follow the logic here.

Interestingly enough, the convertible has the wide, 9.5-inch wheels of the Z51 as standard equipment, which suggests that they have a beneficial effect on ride. Obviously, they don't hurt skidpad adhesion: at 0.85 g, this car's performance is not significantly different from past Corvettes'.

In fact, except for the folding roof, this new Corvette continues much as before. Acceleration is about the same; top speed is down a few mph, to 144, probably because of greater aerodynamic drag over the convertible top. Braking is noticeably better for one or two moderate-speed stops now that the anti-lock system is in place, but the Corvette still shows some fading tendency when the brakes are used aggressively at high speeds. We don't think this will be particularly noticeable in typical American driving—most buyers will probably instead be enthralled by the new anti-lock system—but Chevrolet has some work to do if it expects to match the best brakes available from Porsche and other European makers.

Keen observers will notice that a new logic is operating the manual transmission's electric overdrive. Previously, one flick of the switch would lock out the overdrive forever. Now, if the engine has been off for more than ten seconds or so, the overdrive will automatically be engaged

when the engine is started again. If the driver wants it out, he has to lock it out each time he starts the engine. Corvette engineers were afraid the old system would be considered a "defeat device" by the EPA; with overdrive engaged, fuel economy is improved by 2.5 mpg in the combined test, enough to escape the gas-guzzler tax.

Escaping the tax takes on new importance with the convertible. Its price has not been announced at press time, but Chevrolet spokesmen estimate a $4000-to-$5000 increment over the coupe's price, which means a window sticker solidly in the $30,000 range when the usual options are figured in. That's serious bucks.

And it brings up a serious question. Could a couple of drifters with no visible means of support afford to cruise Route 66 in a Corvette convertible today, the way they did on TV two dozen years ago? Maybe the question is moot, because Route 66 doesn't exist anymore. The federal government, figuring that Interstates handle the traffic now—and, who knows, maybe figuring there would never be another convertible Corvette—decommissioned that famous old highway a few months back, replacing the "66" signs with local route numbers.

So the Corvette convertible is returning to a changed world. The TV networks wouldn't go with Tod and Buz anymore, either. Today's adventurers would be Chip and Buffy, and they'd probably drive an automatic.
                                    —*Patrick Bedard*

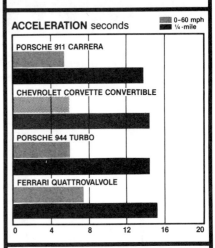

CURRENT BASE PRICE dollars x 1000

PORSCHE 944 TURBO
PORSCHE 911 CARRERA
CHEVROLET CORVETTE CONVERTIBLE (estimated)
FERRARI QUATTROVALVOLE

0 12 24 36 48 60

ACCELERATION seconds

▨ 0–60 mph
■ ¼-mile

PORSCHE 911 CARRERA
CHEVROLET CORVETTE CONVERTIBLE
PORSCHE 944 TURBO
FERRARI QUATTROVALVOLE

0 4 8 12 16 20

Vehicle type: front-engine, rear-wheel-drive, 2-passenger, 2-door convertible

Price as tested: $34,500 (estimated)

Options on test car: Delco-GM/Bose sound system, leather seats, power driver's seat, cruise control, power door locks

Standard accessories: power steering and windows, A/C, tilt steering

Sound system: Delco-GM/Bose AM/FM radio/cassette, 4 speakers

ENGINE
Type . . . . V-8, iron block and aluminum heads
Bore x stroke . . . . 4.00 x 3.48 in, 101.6 x 88.4mm
Displacement . . . . 350 cu in, 5733cc
Compression ratio 9.5:1
Engine-control system . . . . GM/Chevrolet Computer
Command Control
Emissions controls . . . . . 3-way catalytic converter, feedback
fuel-air-ratio control, EGR, auxiliary air pump
Valve gear . . . . pushrods, hydraulic lifters
Power (SAE net) . . . . 230 bhp @ 4000 rpm
Torque (SAE net) . . . . 330 lb-ft @ 3200 rpm
Redline . . . . 5500 rpm

DRIVETRAIN
Transmission . . . . 4-speed with electronic overdrive
Final-drive ratio . . . . 3.07:1, limited slip

Gear	Ratio	Mph/1000 rpm	Max. test speed
I	2.88	8.5	47 mph (5500 rpm)
I O.D.	1.93	12.6	38 mph (3000 rpm)
II	1.91	12.8	70 mph (5500 rpm)
II O.D.	1.28	19.0	105 mph (5500 rpm)
III	1.33	18.3	101 mph (5500 rpm)
III O.D.	0.89	27.4	123 mph (4500 rpm)
IV	1.00	24.4	122 mph (5000 rpm)
IV O.D.	0.68	35.8	144 mph (4000 rpm)

DIMENSIONS AND CAPACITIES
Wheelbase . . . . 96.0 in
Track, F/R . . . . 59.6/60.4 in
Length . . . . 176.0 in

Width . . . . 71.0 in
Height . . . . 46.6 in
Frontal area . . . . 19.3 sq ft
Ground clearance . . . . 4.7 in
Curb weight . . . . 3266 lb
Weight distribution, F/R 50.2/49.8%
Fuel capacity . . . . 20.0 gal
Oil capacity . . . . 4.5 qt
Water capacity . . . . 14.6 qt

CHASSIS/BODY
Type . . . . full-length frame integral with body
Body material . . . . fiberglass-reinforced plastic

INTERIOR
SAE volume, front seat . . . . 49 cu ft
trunk space . . . . 4 cu ft
Front seats . . . . bucket
Seat adjustments . . . . fore and aft, seatback angle,
front height, rear height
General comfort . . . . poor fair good **excellent**
Fore-and-aft support . . . . poor fair good **excellent**
Lateral support . . . . poor fair **good** excellent

SUSPENSION
F: . . . . ind, unequal-length control arms, plastic
leaf spring, anti-roll bar
R: . ind; fixed-length half-shaft, 2 lateral links, and 2 trailing
links per side; plastic leaf spring; anti-roll bar

STEERING
Type . . . . rack-and-pinion, power-assisted
Turns lock-to-lock 2.5
Turning circle curb-to-curb . . . . 40.4 ft

BRAKES
F: . . . . 11.5 x 0.8-in vented disc
R: . . . . 11.5 x 0.8-in vented disc
Power assist . . . . vacuum with anti-lock control

WHEELS AND TIRES
Wheel size . . . . 9.5 x 16 in
Wheel type . . . . cast aluminum
Tires . . . . Goodyear Eagle VR50, P255/50VR-16
Test inflation pressures, F/R . . . . 30/30 psi

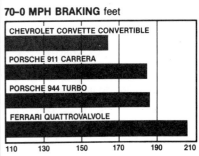

70–0 MPH BRAKING feet

CHEVROLET CORVETTE CONVERTIBLE
PORSCHE 911 CARRERA
PORSCHE 944 TURBO
FERRARI QUATTROVALVOLE

110 130 150 170 190 210

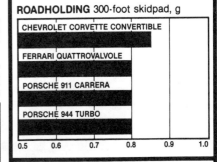

ROADHOLDING 300-foot skidpad, g

CHEVROLET CORVETTE CONVERTIBLE
FERRARI QUATTROVALVOLE
PORSCHE 911 CARRERA
PORSCHE 944 TURBO

0.5 0.6 0.7 0.8 0.9 1.0

CAR AND DRIVER TEST RESULTS

ACCELERATION
	Seconds
Zero to 30 mph	2.0
40 mph	3.1
50 mph	4.4
60 mph	6.0
70 mph	8.1
80 mph	10.2
90 mph	13.3
100 mph	16.4
110 mph	20.6
120 mph	27.3
130 mph	38.3
Top-gear passing time, 30–50 mph	5.0
50–70 mph	4.9
Standing ¼-mile	14.5 sec @ 95 mph
Top speed	144 mph

HANDLING
Roadholding, 300-ft-dia skidpad . . . . 0.85 g
Understeer . . . . minimal **moderate** excessive

BRAKING
70–0 mph @ impending lockup . . . . 164 ft
Modulation . . . . poor fair good **excellent**
Fade . . . . **none** moderate heavy

COAST-DOWN MEASUREMENTS
Road horsepower @ 30 mph . . . . 6 hp
50 mph . . . . 15 hp
70 mph . . . . 33 hp

FUEL ECONOMY
EPA city driving . . . . **17 mpg**
EPA highway driving . . . . **24 mpg**
C/D observed fuel economy . . . . **14 mpg**

INTERIOR SOUND LEVEL
Idle . . . . 56 dBA
Full-throttle acceleration . . . . 84 dBA
70-mph cruising . . . . 77 dBA
70-mph coasting . . . . 77 dBA

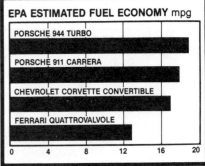

EPA ESTIMATED FUEL ECONOMY mpg

PORSCHE 944 TURBO
PORSCHE 911 CARRERA
CHEVROLET CORVETTE CONVERTIBLE
FERRARI QUATTROVALVOLE

0 4 8 12 16 20

New: Chevrolet Corvette roadster

Return of the convertible 'vette

The Corvette roadster returns to the USA next month, but it could be a brief appearance

by Jeff Brown

THE LAST Corvette soft-top hit the US streets 10 years ago, when consumerism and increasing safety legislation was expected to spell the end of open air motoring. But a return to sanity in the USA's car safety laws has allowed the topless 'vette — a proper Corvette roadster, built by Chevrolet at its Bowling Green, Kentucky, plant — to begin rolling off the production lines as this issue of Modern MOTOR goes on sale. It will be on US showroom floors in February. The bad news for Corvette fanciers is that only 6000 roadsters will be built in the '86 model year.

The Corvette roadster will also be the Indianapolis 500 pace car — without the usual pace car dress-up gear — and this is expected to add even more impetus to the rush for the new soft-top.

The roadster uses the latest version of the Chev 350 small block — 5.7 litres in the new money — and the roadster gets aluminium heads, with compression ratio lifted from 9.0:1 to 9.5:1, larger inlet ports, sintered metal valve seats, and centrally located copper core spark plugs. The new heads (only on the roadster — the coupe keeps the iron heads) also take 18 kg from the engine's weight. Peak power 172 kW at 4000 rpm and pe torque is 447 Nm at 3200 rp The Bosch fuel injection is u changed and there's a new d exhaust system with thr monolith catalytic converter

The roadster gets a standa four speed automatic gearb

and a no cost option is a four speed manual with overdrive on the top three gears (making seven speeds all-up!). It also gets Bosch ABS II anti-lock brakes and uni-directional Goodyear Eagle 255/50VR-16 tyres, on 16 x 8.5 alloy wheels. Cars with the optional Z51 handling pack get 9.5 rims.

Minor changes include tilting the instrument panel to reduce glare, the introduction of optional electric air conditioning and the government-mandated central stop light is mounted high in the middle of the tail.

The Corvette is also the first GM car to get VATS — GM's Vehicle Anti Theft System, which utilises a small pellet in the ignition key which creates an electronic code. If the key code doesn't match that of the car's hidden decoder, it cuts off the starter motor and fuel injectors. There are also sensors in the doors, bonnet and boot, and GM says it will take even experienced thieves at least half an hour to have a chance of beating the system.

The topless 'vette is much changed under its fibreglass skin: there's an increased diameter bracing tube between the chassis rails in front of the engine; substantially larger braces from the frame rails to the under engine cross member; more front torque box re-inforcement; added cross braces from the door hinge pillars to the rear torque box on the opposite side; a stiffened steering column and mounting system; an extra bar across the top of the rear torque box behind the seats; a double panel seat back riser for extra cross-car stiffness; and an aluminium frame for the convertible top.

Suspension changes include a 10 mm ride height increase to restore ground clearance lost to the extra cross bars; a drop in recommended tyre pressure from 35 to 30 psi; GM's first use of its new "deflected disc" shock absorbers; and restrictors in the power steering lines to dampen torsional steering shake.

The manually operated convertible top is raised or lowered in a simple, three step sequence and is stowed out of sight under an electrically operated panel behind the seats. When the panel is opened the top is released and is then pulled forward by hand and connected by two latches above the sun visors. The inside of the roof is velour lined.

Price of the Corvette roadster had not been announced as we went to press, but to the 6000 potential owners of the 1986 model run, we doubt that the price will mean anything . . .

CALLAWAY TWIN-TURBO CORVETTE

(Connecticut) Yankee ingenuity makes America's only sports car fast—and we mean really fast

IF THE WORLD were a perfect place and logic always prevailed, automotive enthusiasts en masse would ungrudgingly accord the Chevrolet Corvette the praise it deserves. After all, here is a world-class sports car designed and built in (dare we say it?) America! Looks terrific. Handles great. Goes like stink.

When Chevy's chief engineer Don Runkle says, "If it won't do 150 mph, bring it back," he's not joking. The Vette is an honest century-and-a-half tourer. But does that satisfy the malcontents amongst us? No-ooo.

Knowing that a Corvette can pull more than 0.9g on the skidpad, that its engine management system and multiple-point fuel injection are among the most sophisticated in the industry, that its ABS will allow you to stop quickly and easily on a curve in the wet, nitpickers cite the obvious. To wit: A Vette is not a true world-class car because it's not as fast as a Ferrari or a Lamborghini.

Lesser principals than Dave McLellan, chief of the Corvette group, would probably ignore this criticism. But McLellan and company believe that the best defense is a good offense, which explains why they called on the turbocharging talents of the

Reeves Callaway organization and came up with a factory-approved, fully warrantied package that makes the 1987 Corvette not just as fast, but faster than exotics such as the Lamborghini Countach, the Ferrari 3.2 Mondial, 328 GTS and 412. True, the Callaway Twin-Turbo Corvette isn't quite as fast as the GTO and the Testarossa—both do about 180 mph while the Vette goes only 178. But the GTO and Testarossa cost $175,000 and $102,500, respectively, while the Vette costs about $51,000. And there's no question about legality, not to mention driveability, serviceability and durability. "We want this to be a 50,000–100,000-mile car and we don't want an owner to have to make any concessions because it's turbocharged," says Tim Good, Callaway Turbosystems' project engineer.

To ensure such longevity, the Callaway Twin-Turbo Vette uses Chevrolet's LF5 truck block with 4-bolt main bearings and forged crankshaft (the standard Corvette crank is cast iron), forged connecting rods and Callaway-designed Cosworth pistons with a 7.5:1 compression ratio. The mains are align-honed and all applicable bits are balanced and blueprinted. Standard Corvette aluminum cylinder heads and a Vette camshaft are used in order to meet

emissions regulations. Purpose-built headers channel exhaust gases to the turbochargers (with wastegates) and into the dual warm-up catalysts that feed a single underbody cat. All very neat—and very legal.

The muscle behind the Twin-Turbo Vette's speed and performance is the Callaway-designed turbocharging system that uses a pair of IHI model RHB52W water-cooled center section turbos and twin air-to-air intercoolers. Fed by special, hood-mounted ductwork that draws its intake air from large NACA ducts, the two blowers provide 10–12 psi of boost pressure and raise horsepower from 230 to 345 bhp at 4000 rpm and increase torque from 330 lb-ft at 3200 rpm to 465 lb-ft at 2800 rpm, more than the legendary 1968 L88 Corvette (R&T, February 1986). "We wanted to give the 350-cu-in. Small Block the feeling of a 454-cu-in. Big Block," says Good, who points out that even at 1900 rpm, the Callaway Twin-Turbo develops 400 lb-ft of torque. What it all means is that instead of shifting gears, one has only to step lightly on the throttle for immediate (and strong) acceleration.

Callaway has retained the Corvette's engine-management system right down to the knock sensor. Ditto, the standard fuel injection. "It's a fantastic thing that we didn't want to reinvent, so we left it alone," says Good, who explains that the only significant change to the stock Rochester setup is the addition of Callaway's Micro Fueler II, which provides auxiliary fuel enrichment to compensate for the extra volume of air being pumped in by the turbos.

Gearbox and driveline are stock, a testimonial to the Corvette's inherent sturdiness. "Chevy assured us that the power we were projecting would not present any problems," claims Good. Nor are there any changes to the optional, factory-installed Z51 Corvette suspension and brakes. In fact, the only visual clues to the car's nature are the in-hood NACA ducts, the specially crafted Callaway intake plenum, Callaway badges on the sides and rear of the bodywork and a boost gauge on the instrument panel.

If this seems a bit understated for a car of this performance level (a Countach is garish by comparison), it's because Chevrolet prefers it that way. Research has shown that while the performance buffs want to go as radical as possible, the conservatives among Corvette owners don't like ostentation. So the Twin-Turbo Vette is the best of both worlds—a radical car that looks essentially stock. And runs that way too. At least until you tip into the throttle. That's when things begin to happen—fast. From a standstill, 60

mph is just 5.0 seconds away; the quarter mile, 13.7 sec. (If you keep the coolant temperature from climbing above 200 degrees and speed shift like Corvette engineer Jim Ingle, those times drop to 4.6 and 13.0 sec, respectively.) Equally impressive is the extremely smooth transition from off-boost to full boost acceleration which occurs at approximately 1300 rpm. Full throttle presses you firmly and steadily into the seat's back cushion, almost from the word go (unlike the acceleration of a certain German turbocar which is first lullaby soft, then Wagner *fortissimo*). You'll note from the data panel that initial acceleration can lag the stock product slightly—owing to the 7.5:1 compression ratio, but believe us, it's hardly noticeable. For those who have the inclination, time and distance, there's that incredible top speed, 177.94 mph, as measured by the electronic timer at Ohio's Transportation Research Center where we conducted the high-speed phase of our test. At TRC, Reeves Callaway, as well as our "Speed" Simanaitis, repeatedly circled the plant's 7.5-mile oval at speeds in excess of 175 mph. The Vette never dropped a stitch. When testing was done, Callaway and Tim Good threw their luggage into the Twin-Turbo prototype and headed back for Connecticut. Try that with some of your high-dollar exotics.

Although it's built by Callaway, the Twin-Turbo is considered to be a Chevrolet product, available from selected dealers as RPO B2K and priced at $19,900 plus the cost of the car. After you order your car, Chevrolet builds it and ships it to Old Lyme, Connecticut where Callaway technicians replace the stock powerplant with the twin turbo. You pick up the car in Connecticut or Callaway delivers it to you personally (no need to worry about some flat-rater taking a few hot laps in your baby while heading for a cup of Joe and crullers at the local Mister Donut). Of course, even the best can break down and it's reassuring to know that the Callaway Twin-Turbo Corvette is covered by a full factory warranty.

Although Callaway hopes to fill the pipeline with cars (the initial build is one per week, but ultimately that's expected to increase to about 250 cars per year), the nation's roadways will not suddenly be overflowing with Callaway Twin-Turbos. "This is not a car for the guy who can't decide between a Testarossa and a Countach," says Good. "Rather, it's a car aimed at those individuals who don't care what it says on the outside. They simply want to have the fastest, best-handling, best-braking car they can buy. We're able to give it to them. We're also proud because it's American-made."

Fast enough to be a real Testa roaster or to send a Lamborghini down for the Count.

PRICE

	Callaway Corvette 1986	Chevrolet Corvette 1986
List price, FOB Detroit		$27,405
Price as tested	est $50,865	$30,965

Price as tested includes std equip (air cond, elect. window lifts, elect. adj mirrors); Callaway turbocharged engine and accessories (est $19,900), AM/FM stereo/cassette ($895), sunroof ($615), Z51 susp ($470), leather seats ($1025), misc options ($555)

ENGINE

Type	turbocharged ohv V-8	ohv V-8
Bore x stroke, mm	101.6 x 88.4	
Displacement, cc	5733	
Compression ratio	7.5:1	9.5:1
Bhp @ rpm, SAE net	345 @ 4000	230 @ 4000
Torque @ rpm, lb-ft	465 @ 2800	330 @ 3200
Fuel injection	Bosch multi-point	
Fuel requirement	unleaded, 91 pump oct	

GENERAL

Curb weight, lb	est 3430	3280
Test weight	est 3600	3450
Weight dist (with driver), f/r, %	est 52/48	51/49
Wheelbase, in.		96.2
Track, front/rear		59.6/60.4
Length		176.5
Width		71.0
Height		46.7
Trunk space, cu ft		11.6
Fuel capacity, U.S. gal.		20.0

DRIVETRAIN

Transmission	4-sp manual + OD
Gear ratios: 4th (1.00)	3.07:1
3rd (1.33)	4.08:1
2nd (1.91)	5.86:1
1st (2.88)	8.84:1
Final drive ratio	3.07:1

CHASSIS & BODY

Layout	front engine/rear drive
Body/frame	fiberglass/skeletal steel
Brake system, f/r	11.5-in. vented discs/ 11.5-in. vented discs, pwr assist, ABS
Wheels	alloy; 16 x 9½
Tires	Goodyear Eagle VR-50, P255/50VR-16
Steering type	rack & pinion, pwr assist
Turns, lock-to-lock	2.0

Suspension, f/r: upper and lower unequal-length A-arms, transverse fiberglass leaf spring, tube shocks, anti-roll bar/upper & lower trailing arms, lateral arms, tie rods, halfshafts, transverse fiberglass leaf spring, tube shocks, anti-roll bar

CALCULATED DATA

Lb/bhp (test weight)	10.4	15.1
Bhp/liter	60.2	40.1
Engine revs at 60 mph in top gear		1650
R&T steering index		0.80
Brake swept area, sq in./ton	184	192

ROAD TEST RESULTS

ACCELERATION

Time to distance, sec:
0–100 ft	3.1	3.0
0–500 ft	7.7	7.7
0–1320 ft (¼ mi)	13.7	14.4

Speed at end of
¼ mi, mph	104.0	96.0

Time to speed, sec:
0–30 mph	2.4	2.1
0–50 mph	3.8	4.4
0–60 mph	5.0	5.8
0–70 mph	6.5	7.7
0–80 mph	8.1	9.5
0–100 mph	12.4	16.2

SPEEDS IN GEARS

Maximum rpm	6000
4th gear	(4855) 178 (4200) 154
3rd	(6000) 98
2nd	(6000) 69
1st	(6000) 46

FUEL ECONOMY

Normal driving, mpg	na	19.0

BRAKES

Minimum stopping distances, ft:
From 60 mph	133
From 80 mph	243
Control in panic stop	excellent
Pedal effort for 0.5g stop, lb	17

Fade: percent increase in pedal effort to maintain 0.5g deceleration in 6 stops from 60 mph ... nil
Overall brake rating ... excellent

HANDLING

Lateral accel, 100-ft radius, g	0.91
Speed thru 700-ft slalom, mph	61.0

INTERIOR NOISE

Idle in neutral, dBA	66	60
Maximum, 1st gear	82	80
Constant 70 mph	79	77

ACCELERATION

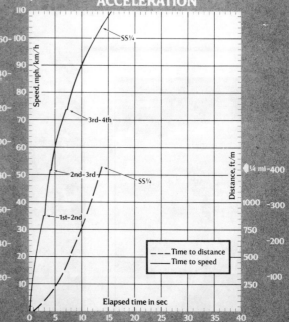

48

Sweet excess, with the factory's blessing.

BY JAMIE KITMAN

TWIN-TURBO CORVETTE

Old Lyme, Connecticut—In automobiling, as in other areas of life, too much of a good thing may in the end be too much. The sweet smell of success, rock star Pete Townshend once observed, is wont to be replaced by the stale odor of excess. So true.

But Townshend obviously wasn't thinking about the latest development from General Motors and the turbomeisters at Callaway Turbosystems. A Chevrolet Corvette equipped with a pair of turbochargers, this muscular slingshot is success and excess rolled into one fine-smelling package. When it goes on sale late this year at selected Chevy dealerships across the country, it will be the fastest and most accelerative car available in America. With a scheduled price lower than that of a stock Porsche 928, the twin-turbo Corvette will, in addition, have made the cost of excess just a little less excessive.

There is a theory behind this car, an immodest philosophy that Callaway project engineer Tim Good expresses: "Quickest. Fastest. Relatively inexpensive [at approximately $50,000]. And, it's American. This is rolling patriotism at its finest."

Clearly, the principals needn't have bothered with a marketing survey before hatching this project. Mind-searing performance is a timeless sort of idea; the twin-turbo Corvette is an instant classic, a machine bound to appeal to a small but significant segment of the market. That segment? Rich maniacs. To which one who had just driven the beastie might add: And may God bless 'em.

You've heard of the Callaway operation before, tucked away here in Old Lyme (203–434–9002). The company was among the first aboard the aftermarket turbo bandwagon a dozen years ago. That was when many of us thought turbocharging had arrived from the heavens to plant hair on the chest of everything with wheels, requiring just household tools, and with few untoward consequences. All for just pennies a day. Aftermarket suppliers were happy to oblige a burgeoning demand, but the reality didn't prove as happy as had been hoped.

Faulty engineering, poor-quality manufacturing, and consumer stupidity shortened the life of many a loyal powerplant. Awash in warranty claims and unsold turbo kits, most companies withered and died.

But not Callaway. Specializing in turbo conversions for four-cylinder VWs and BMWs, the firm prospered as a result of superior engineering and fastidious attention to detail. From a humble beginning out back of proprietor Reeves Callaway's ancestral home, it grew into a spacious and well-equipped plant erected close by. From these doors today goes forth a steady stream of twin-turbo 928s, Alfa GTVs, and other delectables.

The company's progress through the years was not lost on the Corvette's tenders at General Motors. They'd been flirting with the idea of moving the corporate flagship upscale since the day of its reincarnation in model year 1984. Why couldn't GM's best be one of the world's best? Such a goal would now require neither fraud nor fancy, since the Corvette was no longer an ill-mannered brute that came to pieces when the road started to bend. World-class performance was within its grasp. But a couple of items had to be attended to first.

Job numero uno in the gentrification process would be remedial, a much needed sorting of the car's capable but bone-jarring suspension. As Chevrolet now admits, the original ride and handling balance on the new-generation models was more of an agreement to disagree than a compromise. The 1987 Corvette that provides a base for the Callaway car still posts its predecessor's phenomenal lateral acceleration figures, and today's model rides firmly too. But not too firmly, forgoing the risk of chronic impaction of its occupants' vertebrae. It is a major improvement.

Developments elsewhere on the chassis, if less urgently required, are likewise salutary. Although the original four-wheel-disc braking system had no discernible vices, the 1986 introduction of Bosch anti-skid braking enhanced safety appreciably, bringing with it a measure of Yuppie cachet, deserved for once, as ABS is a truly useful piece of technology.

Step two of the Great March Forward took GM straight into the engine bay. No sane person ever accused a Corvette of sloth, and with 230 bhp and 330 pounds-feet of torque available to motivate its 3250 pounds in stock trim, the 1987 model does not lack spirit. But everyone knows the universal language of car snobs. Nothing adds breeding faster than exclusive performance.

The Corvette is being readied to feature the new 32-valve, 420-bhp V-8 that the General acquired when it purchased Lotus. But even optimists say this exotic touch won't arrive for years. So GM looked around. It liked the work Callaway had done with Alfa Romeo. So, last fall, someone placed a discreet call to Connecticut. The result, pictured on these pages, is anything but discreet.

Consider, for instance, the twin-turbo Corvette's run from 0 to 60. It consumes a mere 4.6 seconds. A trip down to a mailbox precisely one-quarter of a mile away will occupy 13.2 seconds, by which time you'll be traveling 109 miles per hour. According to Callaway, if your mailbox is 175 miles away, this car will get you to it in one hour, conditions permitting. Special delivery indeed.

Acceleration figures like these all but guarantee the twin-turbo Vette the top banana's spot on North American highways. They also guarantee a ready market, but Callaway plans to unleash just 50 to 100 of these devices each year. True to its

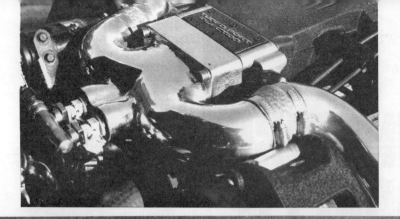
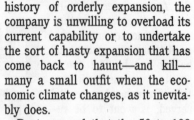

history of orderly expansion, the company is unwilling to overload its current capability or to undertake the sort of hasty expansion that has come back to haunt—and kill—many a small outfit when the economic climate changes, as it inevitably does.

Rest assured that the 50 to 100 people who pony up the bucks will be reveling in their good fortune. All they need to do is purchase a Corvette at one of approximately thirty approved dealerships (prices begin around $27,000) and select the $19,995 Callaway twin-turbo option. After their dream Vette is otherwise dressed to taste, it will be trucked to Callaway's Connecticut plant. There the transformation will begin.

The first thing changed in the Callaway program is the Corvette's standard engine block. The car's camshaft and new-for-1986 aluminum heads are retained, but for extra durability, Callaway prefers General Motors' fortified LT5 truck block, with its steel crankshaft and four-bolt main bearing caps, NASCAR-prepped. Cosworth forged pistons, with Callaway-machined crowns, provide a 7.5:1 compression ratio, down from the standard Corvette's 9.5:1, to reduce the likelihood of detonation. A heavy-duty Melling 55A oil pump is installed for good measure, and the whole assemblage is balanced and blueprinted.

Now comes the really fun stuff, in the form of twin Warner-Ishi IHI RHB52W turbos, with water-cooled center bearings, specially designed for the application and set to provide a maximum boost of 10 psi. The decision to use two smaller turbo units rather than one large one was simple, based on the comparative ease of plumbing and the better throttle response the small-bore puffers offer.

In accordance with the best modern practice, dual air-to-air intercoolers of Callaway manufacture chill the air heated by pressurization. The Corvette's standard fuel-injection system is retained in the interests of emissions control (along with stock valve timing) but is supplemented with the Callaway-designed Microfueler riding under the dash to

PHOTOGRAPHY BY GREG JAREM

supply a richer mixture under boost conditions.

The invigorated Callaway motor is tastefully topped with chromed turbo plumbing, black crinkle-finished valve covers and plenum, and polished aluminum for the intercoolers and the rest of the inlet tract. These complement what must already be one of the most appealing underhood views available, contrasting particularly well with the Corvette's forged-alloy suspension parts.

Air sniffers will appreciate how all stock emissions equipment has been retained, including the full catalyst system, permitting Callaway to receive small-volume-manufacturer certification from the EPA. Interestingly, the combined muffling action of the turbos and the catalyst eliminates the need for additional silencing, allowing straight pipes out the rear. The company's biggest regret, engineer Good reports, is that the car doesn't have a more commanding exhaust note. "But we're working on it," he promises.

Callaway's ministrations underhood deliver a ripsnorting 345 horsepower, with 465 pounds-feet of torque available at 2800 rpm. One might expect exoticar headaches and temperamental behavior with statistics like these, but no. Callaway technicians designed the package with reliability, simplicity of maintenance, and around-town tractability—the basic American car virtues—in mind.

In practice, this motor represents a marriage of modern electronic management systems and classic American hot-rod technique. The union appears to be a happy one. On our test day, the Connecticut air hung heavy at ninety degrees by ten a.m., and the humidity was downright mucilaginous. Once, we walked away in search of a soda pop, only semi-inadvertently leaving the Vette behind idling with both the air conditioning and the Delco/Bose four-speaker stereo fully cranked. Twenty minutes later, there was nary a hiccup from the burbling monster as we set off to roll away the stone.

A punishing day of acceleration runs, high-speed cruising, and casual dawdling didn't dispel our confidence in the motor. (GM is confident enough to warrant the cars.) We had

no confidence in Callaway's claim of 20 mpg highway fuel economy, though, so we weren't surprised to find that driving the bejeezus out of the Corvette caused it to snarfle gasoline at the rate of 13 mpg.

In external appearance, the twin-turbo Vette is virtually indistinguishable from the factory's standard offering; only a boost gauge built into the dash (in a spot formerly occupied by a vent outlet) and a pair of functional NACA ducts, neatly grafted into the hood to feed the intercoolers, tip off cognoscenti to the evil lurking within. On the road, few other Corvette drivers spot the difference, until you apply lots of pedal. Then they know there was something different about that Vette.

By design, torque is the language that the Callaway Vette speaks. The car will pull away smartly from 1200 rpm in overdrive fourth, making shifting with the car's standard four-plus-three manual gearbox virtually optional. While one is notified in no uncertain terms when the turbos start to do the *ha-cha-cha*, bottom-end ergs tide things over until the turbines get up to speed. Full-bore acceleration proceeds in two steps: it is rather like riding a rocket off the pad and then having the second stage boot you up toward escape velocity.

Low-end torque and the potential ability to avoid shifting are, in a sense, a blessing, for the Corvette gets poor marks in and around the transmission tunnel. The standard-issue shifter is balky and unpleasant to use, the sensation of its throw being comparable to that of drawing a sharp butter knife through warm concrete. The overdrive unit—working on the top three gears and operated by a button on the shift knob—kicks in with a jolt and leaves with another. The whole feeling is one of distracting crudity, cheapness even. There is no question, mercifully, about the strength of the box itself.

Callaway found it could handle a couple hundred more horsepower than the turbocharged 350 engine feeds into it.

So it is for the rest of the car. The twin-turbo Vette brings the standard Corvette virtues and vices along for every ride. Ultimate roadholding ability is prodigious on the standard-issue sixteen-inch, asymmetrically vented wheels and 255/50VR-16 gatorbacks. The chassis, including the brakes, seems capable of handling the extra poke. But faults persist. Despite the improved ride, the car has unsatisfactory ground clearance for use on the road. It will drag its front spoiler on a bottle cap. The fiberglass body, meanwhile, has an irritating tendency to creak around town and flap in the breeze at speed. Particularly enervating was the incessant hammering of our test car's fuel filler lid directly aft of the rear hatch at speeds over 120 mph.

Such quibbles—and others in regard to build quality, digital speedos, and the sort of interior plastic that gave plastic a bad name—are singularly, magnificently irrelevant when one enters the turbo zone. Then, the Callaway Corvette seems almighty. Excess incarnate, it makes all other cars seem like Grandma's Deux Chevaux.

Some people might not understand this expression of infinite performance reserve, much less the concept. Others might have ethical problems with it. But what about you? Are you the kind of person who would buy a 35,000-BTU air conditioner from a pizzeria to cool off your bedroom on a hot day? Are you the sort of soul who absolutely requires every single one of the 1731 stations that your satellite dish brings in? Did you ever just feel like ordering everything on the menu, for yourself?

Don't apologize. Buy this car. Slip it into overdrive fourth at 100, where it will pull a serene 3000 rpm, and try to look relaxed. Turn on the Delco/Bose and locate a Mozart concerto or, if you prefer, Ozzy Osbourne's latest. And then breathe deep. Excess rarely smelled better.🛑

Jamie Kitman, a New Jersey lawyer and journalist and a frequent contributor to the Nation, *is partial to British cars (witness his Lotus Elan S4 roadster and Rover 2000TC), baseball, and Rheingold beer.*

Vette Variations

*Three suspension choices tailor the Corvette for everybody
from boulevard cruisers to racetrack warriors.*

• Sports cars aren't meant to be all things to all people. Most of the time, their manufacturers try to please the serious hotshots and leave it at that. The wimps and poseurs who buy their cars can either learn to put up with the discomforts of sports machinery or swallow their pride and shop elsewhere in the future.

Life is less simple for the engineers responsible for the Chevrolet Corvette. As the guardians of the world's least expensive and best-selling 150-mph car, they have to satisfy a broad spectrum of buyers, from suburban shoppers to Showroom Stock racers. Chevrolet tries to meet their needs by making numerous options available to them, allowing each customer to tailor his car to his particular demands. The problem is getting the buyers to select the appropriate options. All too many Corvette owners wind up gritting their teeth from pothole to pothole because they made the mistake of checking every option in the order book—including the

Z51 competition suspension.

Responding to complaints of ride harshness, the Corvette engineers have tamed both the base suspension and the Z51 option over the past few years by systematically reducing their spring rates. For 1987, they have taken the process a step further with the introduction of a third suspension choice, called Z52. To evaluate precisely the pluses and minuses of the three distinct setups, we ordered a trio of new Corvettes, each equipped with different underpinnings, and put them through their handling paces.

Regardless of the suspension choice, the Corvette's basic hardware is the same. Unequal-length control arms locate the front wheels, and a power-assisted rack-and-pinion mechanism steers them. At the rear is an elaborate five-link design. Exotic plastic leaf springs and conventional anti-roll bars are fitted at both ends. The various components are attached to a welded stamped-steel space frame, and

traction is provided by 255/50VR-16 Goodyear gatorbacks. The suspension geometry and the alignment settings are also common to all three setups.

Beyond these fundamentals, the three Corvette suspensions differ substantially. The base version has relatively soft springs, conventional hydraulic shock absorbers, and tubular anti-roll bars. The steering ratio is a quick 15.5:1, and the big Goodyear rubber is mounted on 8.5-inch-wide wheels.

The next step up is the new Z52 suspension. For an additional $470, you get a solid and thicker front anti-roll bar, Delco/Bilstein gas-charged shocks, a 13.0:1 steering gear, 9.5-inch-wide wheels, and all but one of the chassis stiffeners that shore up the structure of the Corvette convertible. The package also includes an oil cooler, a thicker-core radiator, and a second electric cooling fan. The Z52's spring rates and suspension bushings, however, are identical to those of the base

setup, so this package is still suitable for street use. It offers hard chargers improved handling without the penalty of a buckboard ride.

Comfort is a much lower priority with the Z51 option. Although it has been civilized considerably since it was introduced with the 1984 Corvette, it's still intended primarily for autocrossers and road racers. Priced at $795, it includes all of the Z52 parts, plus substantially stiffer springs, much stiffer lower-control-arm bushings up front, and a solid rear anti-roll bar. To discourage dilettantes from electing this option, it is not available with either the automatic transmission or the convertible body style.

Three distinct personalities were revealed when we compared the suspension packages on and off the test track. On smooth California roads, the base car felt almost plush; its suspension oozed over small bumps and stroked gently over larger ones. The Z52 didn't filter out tiny imperfections quite as well, but the stiffer chassis that comes with the package was definitely a benefit over rougher pavement, practically eliminating the base car's front-end quiver and chassis flex. On most California roads, the two suspensions were about even in comfort, but we know from experience that the Z52 is the better choice for the pockmarked roads of the Midwest.

The Z51 suspension was significantly harsher than the base and Z52 varieties. It wasn't terribly uncomfortable on smooth roads, but the connection between the pavement and the seat was noticeably more direct. On rough roads, we had to push the seatbelt cinch button to keep from being tossed around the cockpit.

The flip side of ride comfort is handling, but we found less difference in our handling tests than we had observed in our ride comparisons. For example, the three Corvettes produced nearly identical skidpad numbers. The base car circulated very neutrally at an impressive 0.86 g. The Z52 Vette felt similar while cornering at 0.87 g. Like the base car, it understeered a

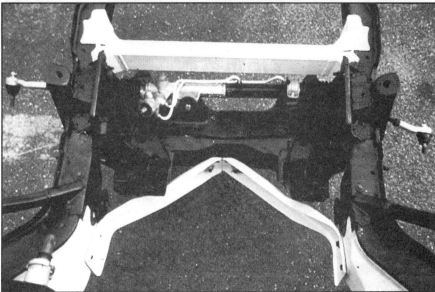

The three Corvettes (top) fought for low-speed-handling honors at the Chrysler Shelby gymkhana course. The chassis reinforcements used on the Z51 and Z52 packages are shown above in white. Both additional braces and double metal layers are used to stiffen the car's front structure.

touch under power, then very gently swung out its tail as we eased off the throttle. In contrast, the Z51 car worked its front tires much harder, and easing off the gas had little effect. It cornered at 0.86 g with much greater understeer.

The stability afforded by understeer is usually an advantage in a slalom course, and this is certainly the case with the Z51 Corvette. Its outstanding 67.5-mph run through our cones required little more than smooth driving; it turned in quickly and precisely and kept its tail neatly in line. The Z52 was a bit slower, mostly be-

cause its tail slid out more easily, though maintaining control was no problem. The base model felt much like the Z52 but turned in less crisply. It was no wallowing wonder, but it couldn't change direction as smartly as the two other cars.

The base car performed better on the autocross course at the Chrysler Shelby California Development Center, in Santa Fe Springs. We found we could slide either end of the car as we desired, and the chassis did a fine job of transmitting the power to the pavement. The Z52 was even quicker; its extra bit of grip and faster

Vital Statistics		spring rates, front/rear, lb/in	anti-roll-bar dia, mm, front/rear	shock absorbers	steering ratio	wheel width, in	chassis stiffeners
	BASE	296/233	26.0 tubular/ 21.8 tubular	Delco standard	15.5:1	8.5	no
	Z52	296/233	30.0 solid/ 21.8 tubular	Delco/Bilstein gas	13.0:1	9.5	yes
	Z51	380/330	30.0 solid/ 22.0 solid	Delco/Bilstein gas	13.0:1	9.5	yes

steering paid off on the twistiest sections of the track. Surprisingly, the Z51 Corvette was the slowest of the group in this test, primarily because its understeer dominated its handling characteristics. Although it was the only car of the three with a manual transmission, we doubt that this was a factor on the relatively low-speed autocross course.

We went to Willow Springs International Raceway for our final test. Instead of running full laps of the course, which would have given a significant advantage to the manual-equipped Z51 Corvette, we limited our timed runs to the twisty section from the entrance of Turn Three to the exit of Turn Six. The Z51 demonstrated its racing bias here in two ways: it turned in the quickest time, and it felt the most comfortable. It was upset by neither the left-right transition nor the downhill braking turn in our test section. We also observed that it felt the most stable in the touchy high-speed entrance to Turn Nine

ger to step out in the turns, and it wouldn't take as clean a set; as a result, extra steering corrections were required. The base car was just as fast in the test section as the Z52, but it felt looser in almost every way. It dived more under braking and tended to drift off the line more. Its chassis, of course, flexed more over bumps, and we could feel its front end moving around during the high-speed entrance into Turn Eight. The base car was still easy to control, but its performance envelope was obviously tighter.

The clear choice for Corvette racers is the Z51 car. Although it was only marginally quicker through the four turns at Willow than the two other cars, it would probably stretch its advantage with the additional grip of shaved Showroom Stock tires. Even on normal tires, the Z51 is by far the most comfortable of the trio on a high-speed track.

On the street, where all three cars have capabilities that go far beyond the limits of

prudence, the choice is more difficult. The Z51, with its mild understeer and tightly controlled body motions, inspires lots of confidence. The Z52 turns in a bit less cleanly and moves around on its suspension more, but the differences aren't great. Factor in its more supple ride and the Z52 is at least as satisfying overall as the Z51 package. The base car's looser structure knocks it back a notch, but we liked its steering best of all. Since 1986, when the caster was increased to six degrees, Corvette steering has had excellent on-center feel and feedback, but the slower ratio of the base car is easier to live with in real-world driving.

If the Corvette suspension options were even broader, we would choose the base setup but substitute the Delco/Bilstein shocks and add the chassis stiffeners. One can order the shock absorbers as an option, but the only way to get the chassis stiffeners with the base suspension is to buy a Corvette convertible. We don't think any Corvette should be without them, because they significantly improve both ride and handling.

Given the options available, our choice for all-around use is the Z52. It provides excellent handling and a good ride, and it works on just about any road surface. On the best roads, the base car rides a bit better than the Z52, without much loss of performance; it's the right choice for cruising Hollywood Boulevard. The Z51 shouldn't be considered for everyday street use, unless you drive only on perfect pavement.

If none of the above strikes your fancy, don't give up hope: seventeen-inch wheels, new tires, and revised suspension geometry are under development for 1988.

—*Csaba Csere*

Test Results		roadholding, 300-ft skidpad, g	maneuverability, 1000-ft slalom, mph	autocross course, sec	racecourse segment, sec
	BASE	0.86	66.1	27.1	20.2
	Z52	0.87	66.9	26.8	20.2
	Z51	0.86	67.5	27.3	20.0

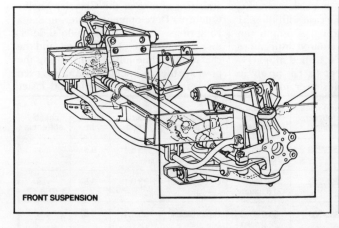

FRONT SUSPENSION

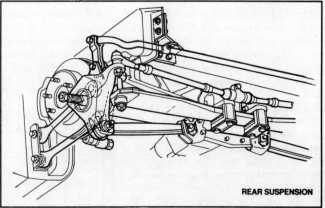

REAR SUSPENSION

GM and Reeves Callaway are experimenting with a waterless cooling system, destined for 1988 twin-turbo Corvettes.

KING OF THE HILL

GM engineers kick out the jams on a Corvette they hope will deservedly be called "the King."

Warren, Michigan—General Motors' Corvette engineers are busy these days. In 1988, the Vette will use computer-controlled shock absorbers developed by Bilstein. The system, like that currently employed on the Porsche 959, isn't as sophisticated as Lotus's active-ride suspension (which won't appear on the Corvette until the 1990s). But Chevy engineers say they are impressed by the Bilstein system's versatility.

The driver manually selects a damping value, depending on the sort of ride he wants. In turn, a computer monitors the shock absorbers through a series of sensors and adjusts them during both compression and rebound. Most such systems adjust during rebound only. The system reacts quickly, about every tenth of a second.

The new Bilstein layout won't be available on early '88 Corvettes because those cars have already been produced. Instead, the system is expected later in the year and is considered an interim measure until the Lotus active suspension is available.

Other Vette improvements on the way include P275/40 seventeen-inch tires, which are already found on the four-wheel-drive, mid-engined Corvette show car. And P315/35 Z-rated tires, good for a sustained 149 mph, are expected by 1990.

Tires with such shallow sidewalls will almost certainly require some sort of active damping.

In the meantime, the Lotus-designed LT5, a 32-valve, 5.7-liter V-8, has undergone tests in a Corvette in Warren. That test mule was also equipped with a six-speed ZF transmission. Producing approximately 350 bhp, according to insiders, the engine is immediately distinguished by sixteen aluminum intake runners leading from the plenum. Says spy photographer Barry Penfound, "By the sound of it, the Lotus motor was pulling cleanly to what I'd guess was around 7500 rpm."

Rumors in Detroit suggest that the Lotus-engined Vette is currently called "the King." It will almost certainly be sold separately from the standard hardtop and convertible models. It is possible that the standard hardtop, some time in the early 1990s, will be fitted with an all-new 4.5-liter, aluminum-block V-8 that will be shared with several other GM cars.

No matter which V-8 appears in upcoming Corvettes, it seems a safe bet that America's sports car eventually will be equipped with Delco Electronics' upcoming traction-control devices. Delco's system limits wheelspin in two ways: brakes are applied to the wheel that is slipping, and a computer reduces engine pow-

er momentarily. Delco expects the system to find a home in a production car by 1990, and "the King" Corvette seems as appropriate a home as any.

But there's even more.

This spy photo of a Corvette LT5 mule shows seventeen-inch tires and wheels. Our photographer says the Lotus V-8 sounds like it "pulls cleanly to around 7500 rpm." The bulge on the hood is thought to be temporarily necessary to clear the sixteen aluminum intake runners.

The National Technologies Hybrid cooling system, which uses a special Dow Chemical–developed waterless coolant, is currently being tested by GM in a Callaway Turbosystems twin-turbo Corvette (where would it receive a more severe test?). The cooling system requires a smaller radiator, and that, in turn, leaves more room for massive turbo intercoolers. The chief advantage of the system is that it allows the engine to operate at

higher temperatures before hot spots and cylinder head cracking appear. "It also delays the onset of pre-ignition," says Reeves Callaway. "And it's particularly useful under what we call an aggravated state—such as if you run 150 mph, turn off the engine immediately, then restart it five minutes later. Usually when you do that, you briefly have an 'air cooled' Corvette—risky business. But that doesn't happen with the new waterless system." As many as 400 Callaway-modified Corvettes may use National's waterless system next year.

Busy, busy bowtie boys.
—Tim Kiska and John Phillips III

Exotic, Erotic Corvettes

**Adding more sex appeal
to Chevy's plastic fantastic**

by Jack R. Nerad

PHOTOGRAPHY BY RANDY LORENTZEN

ince 1953, there has been but one standard bearer of American pride in the ranks of the world's sports cars. Its name, of course, Chevrolet Corvette. For nearly 35 years, it has continued to stave off invasions by the likes of Ferrari, Maserati, Lamborghini, Lotus, and Porsche for sports car supremacy here in the USA. Other domestic marques have dallied in the 2-seater field—Thunderbird, Cobra, AMX, Fiero—but none has captured the imagination of the aficionado in quite the same way as the fiberglass flyer from the bowtie boys.

Sure, the going has not always been easy. In fact, the underpowered, automatic-equipped Cor-

vette of 1953 got off to a stumbling start. Its mild performance did not stir the souls of many Eisenhower-era buyers, and the entire Corvette project was in danger of being scrapped. But, in 1955, performance arrived in the form of the legendary Chevy small block, and the Corvette never looked back. Perhaps no one would have guessed then that same engine would be powering America's premier sports car nearly a third of a century later.

Some might call the pushrod 2-valve Chevy engine low tech, maybe even no tech. No, it's not a high-revving multi-valve buzz bomb of a motor, but to its critics we would say, "Just look at the results." That self-same 30-year-old design is the reason Corvette has made a mockery of its class in showroom-stock endurance racing. It's an ever-reliable torque machine that makes accelerating out of corners a sensual experience. With horsepower ever at the ready, it can turn the wimpiest Don Knotts type into a hero in the stoplight drags. Just put your foot into it and hang on.

But, beyond performance, beyond the simple ability to go, stop, and turn corners with effortless ease, the Corvette has always been something more. It has been a symbol, a talisman, of success, freedom, even virility. That unknown Chevrolet marketing guy who put the Corvette on the "Route 66" TV show succeeded better than he dreamed possible.

The Corvette has always made a statement about its driver. We don't know if there's a "Beretta guy" or a "Honda guy" or even a "Taurus guy," but there can be no doubt there's a "Corvette guy." You can probably picture him in your mind—strong jaw, steely eyes, razor-cut hair, a sort of Malboro Man come to life. Of course, not every Corvette driver fits this description. Hey, some come from the female of the species. But you get the picture. If people "wear" their cars, as the designers would have you believe, then Corvette is a classic American suit of clothes.

That's the other thing about the Corvette since 1955 or so. Not only has it always been able to go like stink, it has also always looked great. Oh, some might decry the abundance of chrome on the '58 model or the

The Vette has been a symbol of success, freedom, and even virility

a series of new ones to be unveiled. It was the reason speculation about a "brand new" Corvette never failed to send car magazine buyers scurrying to their newsstands. Sure, there may have been excesses—styling for styling's sake rather than adherence to the stern dictum, "form follows function." But one thing you could always say about Corvettes: They were never dull.

Throughout the years, there has been a dichotomy within the Corvette ranks. One group might be called the "purists." They could be characterized as following the "Gospel according to Chevrolet." They would sooner stick spikes through their eyeballs than fit one non-factory component on their Corvette. You know this type. They're the ones always checking serial numbers, always inspecting the seat upholstery and the window cranks for telltale signs of non-stock origins, always combing the Corvette

which to begin their search for automotive individuality. This is the group that, in the past, widened fenders to accommodate wider and wider rubber, installed Plexiglas covers over headlight wells, and mounted all manner of spoilers on rear decklids. Many of these exercises proved that beauty, indeed, is in the eye of the beholder, and demonstrated the veracity of the rule that there's no quicker way to lower the value of a Corvette than to modify it. All these excesses, of course, came before the sudden popularity of the European-style "tuner." What many fail to realize is that, for all their high-tech trappings, AMG and the like are nothing more than European hot-rodders. That they are splendid at what they do goes without saying, but we would suggest that having "AMG" cast on a 4-valve head is nothing more than having "ISKY" stamped on a cam. The European tuners' importance to the Corvette story arises because shops like AMG, Alpina, and Koenig have helped legitimize hot-rodding. Suddenly, it has shed its T-shirt-and-Lucky-Strike image and gone uptown. It has helped modified vehicles escape the "Kustom Kar Show" aura and emerge as statements of style and class.

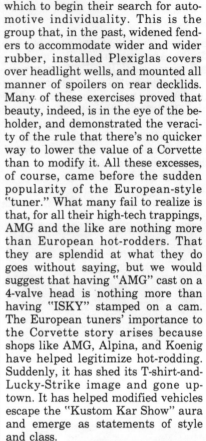

Which brings us to the Corvettes on these pages, Corvettes prepared by several shops that aspire to the status of the top European tuners. Florida is a hotbed of these operations because the climate in Florida, both literally and figuratively, seems right. The Sunshine State has plenty of warm weather to permit year-round top-down tooling, and cash flow doesn't seem to be much of a problem to many South Florida denizens. Of course, there is the red, white, and blue spirit that looks with disdain at foreign machinery, and, finally, there seem to be plenty of individualists who don't want their Corvette to look like everybody else's Corvette. We traveled to Florida to partake of some of the best examples of exotic and erotic Corvettes. What we found were many variations on a single theme, and the theme was, for lack of a better term, "ground-effects." The Corvette tuners have taken a cue from the racing world (and not, coincidentally, from AMG) and have applied wings, airdams, and rocker-panel skirts to provide a more aggressive, individual look to what already is a beautiful design. When Jerry Palmer and his crew laid down the lines in the late '70s and early '80s, they did a masterful job. The best of the tuners' work merely accents those strong points without overwhelming the in-

non-functional side coves from 1956-62 or the bogus hood louvers on the '63 Stingray, but there's no doubt in each new model year that the Vette was an attention-getter. Maybe some purists considered the Corvette too flashy, but if you wanted to make an impact at any '50s, '60s, or '70s party, there was no better car to show up in.

Styling was the reason the pulse quickened when each succeeding model year appeared. It was the reason legions waited breathlessly at their local dealerships for the next in

flea markets for NOS radio antennae and headlight bezels. It is the purists who refer to modified Corvettes as "customs," a word invariably uttered with the derision and contempt one might normally reserve for politicians, arms dealers, or wanna-be actresses with hotpants.

Then there's the other group, who might be called "free spirits." They're unafraid to defy convention and perfectly willing to go where no one has ever gone before. To them, the stock Corvette is just a blank canvas on tegrity of the original.

It is also interesting that most tuners, although they owe their roots to the hot-rod movement, leave the engine and drivetrain pretty much alone. The anti-pollution laws being what they are, messing with the engines of new or nearly new cars can become a rather thankless proposition. They seem content to let the stock setup stand on its own considerable merits, and with 245 hp on tap and 0-60 times in the 6.5-sec range, one really can't blame them. If more power is really necessary, the factory-authorized Callaway Twin Turbo is the option of choice. In this form, horsepower jumps to an estimated 400 and 0-60 times fall below 5 sec. Plenty good, we'd say.

A couple notes before we look at each of the cars individually: First, this is not meant to be an all-inclusive roundup of every Corvette tuner in the country. Second, the quality of workmanship and materials (and the price of the work) varies dramatically. We would strongly suggest that, before you entrust your personal pride and joy to one of these tuners, you inspect several examples of the shop's work. Ask for references and ask about his parts sources. The ease of pulling a fiberglass mold off a given part is such that the field is rife with shoddy quality and counterfeit body pieces. Your best bet is to insist that the tuner deal with parts sources you recognize. Finally, insist that you get an item-by-item rundown of what you're ordering *in writing* and a bottom-line price before the work commences. This may be your only protection against the few fly-by-night operations out there.

The following are some tuners whose work we inspected, drove, and generally messed around with recently:

Quality Motorsports is a Tampa-based firm that specializes in other exotics as well as Corvettes. Their Vette modifications include extensive use of John Greenwood aero pieces like wings, spoilers, and skirts. The model we sampled used all these modifications in paint color-matched to the stock Corvette yellow of the body. The modular Fittipaldi wheels were keyed to the exterior color as well and fitted with Michelin XGT tires. Appearance mods also included blackout taillights and parking lights and attractive Carpathian Elm burl dash appliqués.

In addition to appearance items, Quality Motorsports also undertakes performance modifications. The most popular are exhaust systems and

Most tuners leave the engine and drivetrain pretty much alone, although they owe their roots to the hot-rod movement

shock and anti-roll bar switches. The firm uses either Koni or Bilstein shocks at the owners' discretion. Full conversions are generally completed in 24 to 48 hours. Each project is different, but the price for substantial modifications such as skirts, spoilers, wing, blackout treatments, and dash generally totals about $5000. You, of course, provide the car.

Distinctly Styled Corvettes is another Tampa-based tuner that turns out high-quality work. We had the opportunity to drive three examples from the company, including a striking Callaway Twin Turbo, and left quite impressed with the company's commitment. Like Quality Motorsports, Distinctly Styled Corvettes uses a number of Greenwood components. Special care is used in mating these pieces to the body and color-matching the paint. The company is also noted for individual touches like adding Corvette badges to the targa bar and gold lettering of engine identification.

Distinctly Styled Corvettes often uses BBS component wheels and mates them with Michelin XGT tires. Genuine wood dash panels are also a frequently installed modification. The firm's prices vary considerably since each car is built to the owner's preference. Typical modifications generally run between $2000 and $5000.

Based in Ft. Lauderdale, **Conversion Concepts** caters to a large contingent of South Florida enthusiasts who desire individuality and affordability. The company began as a converter, turning Corvette coupes into

ragtops before the factory-issue convertible was available. Interestingly, the firm remains a strong factor in the Vette convertible business, turning out 400 to 600 copies a year for individuals and dealers across the country. President H.E. "Butch" Hughes claims he can put you at the wheel of a Corvette convertible for as much as $5000 less than Chevrolet can.

Of course, the firm also does extensive modification work, including the installation of several different aero kits. The company also offers blackout treatments, hood louvers, wings, spoilers, and interior modifications. Mild restyling can cost less than $2000, while an extensive project like the conversion of a coupe to a convertible in full aero trim with blackouts, louvers, and modular Epsilon wheels will cost about $40,000, complete. Conversion Concepts vehicles are available at several dealerships around the country under the Carrozza label.

As you can see from the accompanying photographs, the variations available are many. You're limited only by your sense of style and the depth of your wallet. Some might call these cars sacrilegious, but our feeling is, if this is what turns you on, enjoy. Ⓜ

For more information, contact:
Quality Motorsports, Inc.
1101 E. Hillsborough Ave.
Tampa, FL 33604
813/238-8485

Distinctly Styled Corvettes
11408 Wheeling Dr.
Tampa, FL 33625
813/962-3243

Conversion Concepts, Inc.
4491 N.E. 6th Terrace
Ft. Lauderdale, FL 33334
305/561-1113

Ground-effects panels and a subtle, two-tone paint treatment are enough to turn this Vette into a traffic-stopper.

4 SEASONS TEST

CORVETTE ROADSTER

A 23,000-mile year in a great car that's not for everyone.

BY JAMIE KITMAN

Edgewater, New Jersey—The magazine's Four Seasons Chevrolet Corvette roadster rumbled up to my doorstep in the nick of time. The wire that runs inexplicably out of the defroster vent of my Rover (and which turned out to be a hot lead) had touched the cigar lighter, nuking the better portion of the old bird's electrical system. The way it looked, my ride, and my plans for a week's R&R on Dingley Island, Maine, were cooked to a crackly crisp.

Enter the Corvette. What a pleasure it was to see former *Automobile Magazine* computer techie Sarah Deem steam into Edgewater wearing Chevrolet's most deluxe bow tie. She was on her way to nearby Nueva York to start a new life in the employ of the corporate hipsters at *Rolling Stone*, and she had filled the banana yellow Vette to its canvas rafters

with her belongings and had set off from Ann Arbor two days earlier.

Automobile Magazine's editors had provided her with this most distinctive moving van so that I might have one more go at it before its yearlong tenure at 120 East Liberty Street, Ann Arbor, drew to a close. Time flies when you're having fun. Incredible though it seemed, our twelve months with America's only true sports car were just about over. It was time to take stock. And, thanks to Sarah's fortuitous arrival, I'd be able to spend that week in Maine, after all.

For me, the magic carpet ride began the fall before last, when I'd set off from Ann Arbor to inaugurate the Vette's stay with a forty-two-day, 8500-mile tour of North American ballparks (January 1987).

PHOTOGRAPHY BY COLIN CURWOOD

It was in these pages that, shortly after watching the Boston Red Sox go down in flames in the 1986 World Series, I boldly asserted the Corvette was not the world's most brilliant urban transportation concept, but, in my view, it had damned few peers as a transcontinental road gobbler.

Crisscrossing the United States, I became thoroughly enamored of the brute power of its 240-horsepower V-8, its massive roadholding capability, and its relative refinement on the highway. Even before the 1987 models came on line, the bone-crushing ride of earlier Corvettes had been acceptably reengineered.

The tight and professional execution of the droptop conversion also came in for special mention in my January 1987 report, as did the car's respectable fuel economy (an average of 20 mpg), its mammoth four-

wheel discs with anti-lock, and its stone reliability. An oil change was my sole operating expense.

Now, clambering into the Corvette's low-slung cockpit again, all the tactile sensations I had grown to know came back to me, along with memories of my baseball odyssey. I imagined I could almost smell the sportsman's aroma of bratwurst belches and beer exhaust as I twisted the key and lit up the familiar display of glowing digital readouts.

Following its journey from Ann Arbor through the industrial heartland of Ohio, Pennsylvania, and New Jersey, our roadster's sleek and otherwise unblemished fiberglass body carried a layer of gritty road slime. This was to be expected. Still, it had led me to wonder. How had the Vette, once so shiny and new, weathered the intervening months?

Reporting at precisely six months and 12,600 miles (July 1987), associate editor John Stein called it "strong, reliable, and inexpensive to maintain." Warranty repairs (a torn shift boot, a squeaking dashboard, loose seat attachment bolts, and a burned-out turn signal bulb) and $66.48 in scheduled maintenance seemed refreshingly insignificant for a vehicle with supercar capabilities. A good thing it was, too. This car, with its stratospheric $36,750 price, is one Chevrolet that would look particularly foolish if it were anything but dead reliable.

Power-adjusting the charcoal gray leather sport seats as I set out for New England, I noticed the odometer had been run up to 20,000 miles since I'd last seen the car. Surprisingly, the fuel-injected, 350-cubic-inch V-8—a paragon of smooth running when I'd last sampled it—was idling grumpily and stalling easily. And the windshield was cracked in a most peculiar way from a major stone impact that left a series of concentric rings.

"Might this car possibly have been abused?" I said to no one in particular. "Don't be a chump," I corrected myself. "Is the pope Catholic?" The Corvette is endowed with a contagious oversupply of hormones. Of course it's been abused—a spate of boy-racer shenanigans was an absolute certainty each time a new driver signed on. I knew I'd gotten my licks in.

More to the point, I thought, was the question, Might this car be toasted? You know, How much flogging can one piece of plastic withstand before it goes limp?

The short answer is, Quite a bit. On the eve of its return to Chevrolet's central office in Detroit, our Four Seasons Corvette is far from spent. That's a real accomplishment, given the workout it's had. But careful study of its logbook, filled with comments from the Corvette's other handlers, and another 3500 miles behind the wheel of this electrifying rocket ship proved to be illuminating just the same.

At the time of his six-month report, Mr. Stein predicted that we were into a pretty good Corvette, and he was right. At 13,481 miles, the Corvette was returned to the garage to have the shift boot—first replaced at 12,600 miles—correctly installed. The mechanics didn't get it right the first time; somehow, they knocked out the Corvette's overdrive, which is operated by a button on the shift lever. Also, new attachment bolts were installed in the base of the driver's seat, the originals having vanished into thin air. Fortunately, there was no charge for the repairs.

Two and a half months later, with 16,921 miles on the clock, the Corvette went back to the shop with a host of niggling maladies. Now it was time to draw out the billfold in earnest. A pervasive burnt-oil odor was traced to a leaky overdrive pan gasket and a faulty pinion seal; appropriate repairs required more than four hours' labor. A hand brake that could no longer hold the car was adjusted, and a coolant probe that sporadically flashed a warning light was determined to have failed, after a pressure test of the cooling system. The sensor was replaced. With fluid and filter changes, the damage came to $370.93.

My trip to Maine revealed that the Four Seasons Corvette was ready for one final trip to the dealership before going back to Chevrolet. A careful perusal of the car's on-board logbook confirmed this; comments had grown increasingly nasty.

Since the day it arrived, the Corvette was praised by the *Automobile Magazine* staff for the delightful ability and refined manners of its engine. As noted, it needed a tuneup at the end of its year with us, but twenty thousand–plus miles failed to dim our ardor.

Certainly no one begrudges the impending arrival of a 330-horse-power Lotus alloy V-8. But our Corvette was able to start readily in all conditions, including the extreme cold of a Michigan winter, meanwhile delivering an average 19.6 miles per gallon for over 23,000 miles. It stood as a strong counter-argument to those who say the iron-block V-8's day is done.

One sour note under the hood: The logbook shows erratic oil consumption since the car reached the 16,000-mile point. Where it once had been using a quart every 4500 miles, it has recently gone through a quart in 884 miles. A leak of some sort is suspected, although its source is unclear.

As much as we've loved the power and verve of the Corvette, we've consistently been irked by its recalcitrant manual gearbox. Its action improved slightly with use, but the shifter remained a joyless implement to the end, with all the feel, in the words of senior editor John Phillips III, of "a GMC twelve-ton hauler."

A grabby and unusually heavy clutch has been nettlesome, too, as has the jerky actuation of the overdrive. Add the Corvette's hair-trigger throttle and its megawhoopee powerplant to this picture, and you'll soon appreciate that smooth driving can be a chore.

When the Corvette was new, its appalling transmission was a debit

we could live with, but other concerns have surfaced. The ride was always firm, and it still is, but it has begun to feel a bit less controlled. This may be due to wearing shocks and bushings, or suspension alignment that is no longer spot on. And the mild creaking and groaning of the plastic body pieces has become a good bit less mild. As Trant Jarman mused in the log at 19,483 miles, lifting a page from singer Jerry Lee Lewis's book, "There's a whole lotta shakin' goin' on."

On the last run to the shop, a failed power window switch was replaced (a $3.05 part that cost $36.00 to install), and the passenger's power door lock needed attention (a $54.00

REACTIONS
Playing to mixed reviews, but always playing.

For an entire year, as Jamie Kitman pointed out, we wailed, we nailed, and we hammered the Corvette. Yes, we were rude, but as hard as we tried, we couldn't beat our Corvette into submission. I love it.

I love our Vette most with the top down. It's a snap to flop back, so it's one of the most practical convertibles I've ever operated, right in there with the new BMW 325i ragtop. And with the canvas snugged in place, it's the best-looking softtop on the market, an ASC triumph.

We lent the car to Derek Bell for a weekend this past summer, when he was in town for an IROC race. He had a blast and was quite vocal about how well he thought the Vette handled. He had no complaints about its ride, either, but joined us in our condemnation of the clunky shifter. "It's a bit trucklike," he told me, "but one expects that from a big torquey car. One wouldn't say a 928's gearbox is exactly light."

I'll have wonderful memories of the time I've spent in this car and in a prototype yellow Vette convertible. A year after I had borrowed the prototype, Chevy called, asking me where I'd left it when I had finished! If I'd known they were going to be so cavalier about the loan, we'd have had *two* yellow convertibles in our hands all year. Our tough luck.

As far as I'm concerned, anyplace is the right place, and anytime is the right time for a Corvette convertible. And if that means I'm not exactly normal (as Jamie the Bizarre Himself suggests), well, no one's telling me anything I haven't heard before.—Jean Lindamood

Mr. Kitman accuses me of getting up on the wrong side of the bed. Well, maybe. But my wrath built over the course of a full year. Finally it erupted, and I added a chapter in our logbook, titled "Sixteen reasons why I despise this car." That's when I began to wonder whether the Corvette is too perfect a reflection of its country of manufacture. To wit, a place of wild extremes.

The Vette is arguably the best-looking sports car in the world. It wasn't styled for human occupancy, however. The car is harder to climb into than a Ferrari Mondial. With the top in place, visibility is worse than any car this side of a Lamborghini Countach. Nothing with a Samsonite logo will ever find its way into the niggardly cargo bin. The footwell is so cramped that you must rest your left foot *under* the clutch rather than next to it. How is it possible that a 3200-pound car that is fifteen feet long can offer so little usable cabin space?

Oh, boy, Jamie, now you've got me going again.

Shifting gears is like arm-wrestling Rambo. Why does America's greatest sports car offer an absurd push-button overdrive instead of five forward gears? Why can't we hear the costly Delco-GM/Bose stereo? If I drive the Corvette to work in the morning, what do I do if it starts to snow?

There's more to a great sports car than a lissome shape and a sub-six-second 0-to-60-mph time. Has anybody out there noticed that, for $585 more than our Corvette, you can buy a 1988 Porsche 944 Turbo?   —John Phillips III

Living with the Corvette roadster for a full lap of the calendar polarized opinion around the *Automobile Magazine* family. Contributor-barrister Kitman, who logged the most miles in the car, found it thrilling, capable, and rich in character; senior editor Phillips, who has some pretty clear notions about automotive compromise, could find little forgiveness in his heart for the big brute. I guess I fall about midway between these views.

I like the Corvette. I like it a lot. There's a bounce in my step on the way out to drive it, and I always, *always* turn and look at it as I walk away after parking it. I think it's one of the half-dozen best shapes Detroit has ever drawn. I like the close-tailored fit of the cockpit, the kick of the 350 V-8, and the tremendous stick of the giant Goodyears. I like the way it barrels down a winding road at six-tenths, still going faster than many quick cars could at ten-tenths. Yes, I like the Corvette.

On the other hand . . .

It *is* a raucous old bull, one that doesn't show so well when considered as real transportation. Even performance cars must work as *cars*, and although the Corvette is certainly usable in daily running, it's just too coarse and compromised to be much good at it. The ride is still rough and noisy, controls are heavy and vague, the shifter is inexcusable, and—for an automobile of such size and weight—total useful room is silly.

I could say I'd like very much to own a Corvette, but I suppose a truer statement is that I'd like very much to *want* a Corvette.   —Kevin Smith

labor charge). The driver's seat mounting was giving trouble again: An annoying squeak turned out to be a broken bracket ($85.00 in labor and $49.06 in parts). Finally, the right top latch stopped holding the top closed properly, but we fixed it ourselves with a $22.88 latch cover. Replacing the cracked windshield set us back $310.00, but we have not figured that expense as an operating cost: An encounter with a flying stone *can* happen to any car, even if it actually *does* happen to few.

Thumbing through the log, it emerged that John Phillips III was the Corvette's most vociferous critic. In the book, he complained about the Vette's bulk (at more than 3300 pounds, this tight-fitting two-seater is hardly a featherweight); its ineffective wipers (the driver's-side blade no longer clears the top half of the windshield); and the generally poor visibility with the top up.

Reading on, I find he had further objections to the Vette's lack of cargo space, raucous demeanor, and meager grip in slush and snow. Phillips also decried the Chevy's indifferent trim quality. To these, it may be added that the hand brake will need adjustment again soon, and that, while standing in traffic, one frequently catches a whiff of super unleaded.

Mr. Phillips's points are well taken. Still, it's a matter of emphasis. I suspect the intensity of his criticism is a reflection of his having driven the Corvette roadster in the wrong places at the wrong times.

In the dead of winter, or in any other situation when it is not possible to put the power or the top down, one could be forgiven for disliking this car. Although proper Eagle M+S snowshoes tamed it quite a bit during the dark months in Michigan, one still can't take full advantage of the Corvette's great grip and lusty torque for much of the winter. A driver could easily make the mistake of expecting it to behave like a normal automobile.

As we learned during the course of this year, the Corvette roadster most assuredly is not normal. You can't fit much more than Tom McCahill's proverbial six-pack and a pair of socks in it. But the fact is, you can't

roll through South Dakota at 135 miles per hour in a Plymouth Reliant, either. Maybe the Corvette is just not a car for normal people.

Our Four Seasons Corvette was at its absolute best when sailing down a lonely highway at a low-three-figure pace on a mild evening with the top down. Looking back at my calendar, I am reminded that it was my undistilled pleasure to have sampled the Corvette almost entirely this way for most of the 12,000 miles I spent with it. Perhaps this made for myopic perception. But, as far as I'm concerned, this year has been one long season: the right one.

We conclude that a Corvette road-

ster is somewhat impractical as a year-round, only-car proposition. But we wouldn't rule it out for that use. During the past year, we've found ours to be generally reliable and pretty cheap to run. Admittedly, it is not inexpensive to buy, and it may be outdone in value for money. But there's a larger issue here. This yellow Corvette has delivered more fun per mile than just about anything we can think of. No, it's not perfect. But, on our word, the world is a better place for it.

Jamie Kitman, a New Jersey attorney and journalist, is a regular contributor to Automobile Magazine.

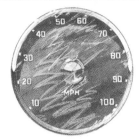

OVERALL RATING

1987 CHEVROLET CORVETTE ROADSTER

We knew the open-air version of America's sports car was gutsy and sure-footed; now we know it's also screwed together pretty well. Living with it day in and day out, some staffers were prepared to forgive its lack of refinement (stiff ride, cramped space, clunky gearbox), and others were not. No argument, however, on two points: The Corvette roadster is fabulous to look at, and it's great fun to drive.

	EXCELLENT	GOOD	FAIR	POOR
ENGINE				●
HANDLING				●
RIDE QUALITY			●	
COMFORT			●	
ISOLATION		●		
BODY INTEGRITY				●
INTERIOR INTEGRITY			●	
RELIABILITY				●

REVIEW PERIOD:
One year
23,273 miles

SCHEDULED MAINTENANCE:
Parts $50.01
Labor $49.41
Fluids $46.54

WARRANTY REPAIRS:
Parts $38.26
Labor $398.10

NONWARRANTY REPAIRS:
Parts $75.49
Labor $213.02

FUEL ECONOMY:
19.6 mpg

RUNNING COSTS (gas, oil added between changes, and nonwarranty maintenance and repairs):
$154.82 per month
$0.079 per mile

PROBLEM AREAS:
Seat mountings
Transmission seal
Convertible top latches
Power window and door lock switches
Dashboard squeaks

ALL THE KING'S HORSES AND ALL THE KING'S MEN

But no King, of the Hill, that is

Okay, so we're suckers for red Corvettes. Red Corvette (foreground) is a stock Z51 with King of the Hill-size rubber (notice the 315/35ZR-17s protruding past the rear fenderwells) and the IMSA GTO body kit (front and rear spoilers, side skirts, rear skirt with exhaust cutouts, hood louvers and extra shark gills). Then, working toward the rear, our stock 1988 Z51 test car, Bakeracing showroom stock car and Morrison/Baker prototype. Enough to play King for a Day.

COMPARISON ROAD TEST R&T

THE RELATIONSHIP BETWEEN the automotive press and the auto companies is a strange Texas two-step. When nothing's happening, everyone dances with you . . . close. But as soon as a particular project gets hot, would-be Fred Astaires suddenly develop two left feet. Or they talk in riddles . . . of cabbages (loquats?) and sealing wax—of Cadillac 12-cylinder engines created from current 4.5-liter V-8s with corporate 2.5-liter inline-4s grafted onto the end. Which end? Either end, it doesn't matter.

The same thing happens when you get close—too close—to information the companies would prefer to keep secret for marketing reasons. Tell everyone about the all-new Flitzmobile coming out in six months, and instantly sales of the current model are deader than the proverbial doornail. At least, that's what the marketeers fear.

Right now at General Motors, any continuation of the market-share slide that started two years ago is to be avoided at all costs. Chevrolet's been bitten by the wait-and-see Corvette buyer more than once. It happened in 1984 when word leaked out that the Vette's lackluster Crossfire throttle-body fuel injection system would be replaced the following year with tuned-port injection. And to a lesser degree, sales dropped a bit in 1985 as potential buyers caught wind of the soon-to-be-introduced roadster.

Such is the case with Chevy's mystery supercar, the King of the Hill Corvette. You've seen the spy photos. You've read the rumors. A few months back we went in search of this elusive Chevrolet. Or at least some key bits and pieces that will likely be part of the package.

Our quest started with what we knew about the KOTH. Limited production for model year 1989. Chevy/Lotus 4-cam, 4-valve-per-cylinder engine, 370–400 bhp, 6-speed transmission, W-I-D-E 17-in. Goodyear Eagle Gatorbacks front and rear, big brakes, revised bodywork and suspension. Expensive. (For more details, see the related story "Gone Kingfishin'.") It progressed to a concept that included testing the best-perform-→

PHOTOS BY JOHN LAMM

ALL THE KING'S HORSES AND ALL THE KING'S MEN

ing current Corvette, a 1988 coupe equipped with the Z51 suspension, big brakes and wheels/tires, manual 4/7-speed transmission and 3.07:1 final drive, along with two other versions with performance characteristics that go several steps above the production model.

In other words, possible precursors to the King.

Corvette engineers have made good use of the SCCA's Escort Endurance series not only to grind Porsche's nose in the Vette's rubber dust but also to test for product development. The big brakes Corvette Escort pilots raced with for a year and a half have become production items in 1988. The weaknesses that engine whiz Kim Baker found in production 350-cu-in. small-blocks, during three years of building engines for the Escort series, were fed back to Chevrolet. Compression-ratio, piston, cylinder head and cam changes incorporated into the current Vette engine all owe their existence to Kim's discoveries and to endurance racing. Ditto suspension improvements. And we have firsthand knowledge of the improvements Goodyear made in its Gatorback tires as a result of the testing and racing it did with Bakeracing these past three years.

Baker's Corvettes have won the Escort series two years running, and even his keenest rivals admit it's more than luck that makes Kim's cars winners. Start with meticulous attention to the tiniest detail in the car as well as the engine. Add the best crew in the business and finish with drivers—such as Tommy and Bobby Archer, Mitch Wright and Kim himself—who know when to go fast and when to slow down. On Kim's dyno, an Escort-prepped small-block cranks out about 325 bhp, a healthy 80-more ponies than the 1988 production Vette. We're creeping into King of the Hill territory.

The third Vette we chose was one that showed up at Nelson Ledges for last year's running of the granddaddy of all 24-hour showroom-stock enduros and simply blew away the competition. This car was a joint effort of Tommy Morrison (car) and Kim Baker (engine). It ran in the prototype class and sported the Corvette IMSA GTO body kit, big brakes at the rear as well as the front and wider wheels and tires than are allowable in the Escort series, Goodyear 275/40ZR-17s vs 255/50ZR-16s. Running as a 1988 prototype, it was entered, aptly, as car No. 88. According to Kim, the engine he built for No. 88 developed

Sporting 360-plus bhp and the 17-in. wheels, front tires and large brakes destined for the 1989 King of the Hill Vette, the No. 88 Morrison/Baker car generated high expectations.

something like 360-plus horsepower. That's comfortably (or uncomfortably, according to which side you're on) close to what Chevy expects the KOTH's 4-cammer to produce.

So with a suitable representation of the King's horses rounded up, we asked a few key members of the King's court to joust: Kim Baker of Bakeracing, Tommy Hart and the Morrison Racing Team and, of course, Chevrolet Product Engineering Manager for Corvette and Camaro, John Heinricy his-self. And off we galloped to GM's desert proving grounds in Mesa, Arizona. There, we'd try the three Vettes on the high-banked 5-mile circular track (first of its kind in the world) for top-speed testing, the west straightaway for acceleration and braking tests, and the 17-acre dynamics pad (the other Black Lake) for skidpad ⟫⟶

> *W*'re creeping into
> *King of the Hill territory.*

A revised camshaft improves engine breathing and nets stock Vettes with the 3.07:1 axle a 5-bhp gain for 1988.

GENERAL DATA

	1988 Chevrolet Corvette Z51	Bakeracing SCCA Escort Corvette	Morrison/Baker Nelson Ledges Corvette
Price			
Base price	$29,480	na	na
Price as tested[1]	$34,034	est $43,000	est $48,000
General			
Curb weight, lb	3330	est 3200	est 3200
Test weight	3440	est 3300	est 3300
Weight dist (with driver), f/r, %	50/50	49/51	49/51
Wheelbase, in.	96.2	96.2	96.2
Track, f/r	59.6/60.4	59.6/60.4	59.6/60.4
Length	176.5	176.5	178.0
Width	71.0	71.0	71.0
Height	46.7	45.7	45.7
Fuel capacity, U.S. gal.	20.0	20.0	20.0
Engine & Drivetrain			
Engine type	ohv V-8	ohv V-8	ohv V-8
Bore x stroke, mm	101.6 x 88.4	101.6 x 88.4	103.1 x 88.4
Displacement, cc/cu in.	5743/350	5743/350	5907/360
Compression ratio, :1	9.5	10.0	10.5
Bhp @ rpm, SAE net	245 @ 4300	325 @ 4400	360 @ 5000
Torque @ rpm, lb-ft	340 @ 3200	410 @ 3250	437 @ 3500
Fuel injection	elect. port	elect. port	elect. port
Transmission	4sp M+OD	4sp M+OD	5sp M
Gear ratios, :1, 1st	2.88	2.88	2.77
2nd (OD)	1.91 (1.31)	1.91 (1.30)	1.88
3rd (OD)	1.34 (0.91)	1.34 (0.91)	1.46
4th (OD)	1.00 (0.68)	1.00 (0.68)	1.19
5th	na	na	1.10
Final drive ratio, :1	3.07	3.07	3.07
Chassis & Body			
Layout	front engine/ rear drive	front engine/ rear drive	front engine/ rear drive
Body/frame	fiberglass/ skeletal steel	fiberglass/ skeletal steel	fiberglass/ skeletel steel
Steering type	rack & pinion, power-assisted	rack & pinion, power-assisted	rack & pinion, power-assisted
Steering overall ratio, :1	13.0	13.0	15.6
Brake system, f/r	13.0-in. vented discs/ 12.0-in. vented discs, vacuum-assist, ABS	13.0-in. vented discs/ 11.5-in. vented discs, vacuum-assist, ABS	13.0-in. vented discs/ 12.0-in vented discs, vacuum-assist, ABS
Wheels	alloy, 17 x 9½	alloy, 16 x 9½	alloy, 17 x 9½
Tires	Goodyear Eagle ZR40, 275/40ZR-17	Goodyear Eagle ZR50 S, 255/50ZR-16	Goodyear Eagle ZR40 S, 275/40ZR-17
Suspension, f/r	upper & lower unequal-length A-arms, transverse fiberglass leaf spring, tube shocks, anti-roll bar/upper & lower trailing arms, lateral arms, tie rods, halfshafts, transverse fiberglass leaf spring, tube shocks, anti-roll bar		

[1]Price as tested includes, for the 1988 Corvette, std equip. (air cond, elect. window lifts, elect. adj mirrors), Z51 suspension package (includes 275/40ZR-17 tires, 17 x 9½ wheels, 13.0-in. front brake discs) $1295, leather seats ($1025), AM/FM stereo/cassette ($773), removable roof ($615), 6-way pwr seats (upgrade) $480, rear window heat ($165), temp control (upgrade) $150, vanity mirror ($51); for the Bakeracing Corvette, race prep (includes rebuilt engine, 13.0-in. front brake discs, suspension adjustment, roll cage, 2-way radio); for the Morrison/Baker Corvette, race prep (includes engine: bored-out cylinders, forged steel crankshaft, ported heads, larger injectors, race camshaft and valve springs, forged pistons, roller rocker arms, tuned intake and exhaust; roll cage, GTO body kit, plastic rear window).

ALL THE KING'S HORSES AND ALL THE KING'S MEN

work. Then, at nearby Firebird International Raceway, we'd get in some 700-ft slalom runs and a few hot laps around its 1.5-mile road course.

When the tire, brake and clutch dust (and more Arizona dust than we'd have liked) settled, it was time to crunch the numbers and see if our instincts were right. Were the pumped-up, hunkered-down Baker and Morrison race cars the stuff Kings would be made of? Was the 1988 Z51, with its front tires, wheel diameter, brakes and suspension destined for Corvette coronation, a measurable improvement over past-model Z51s?

You'll recall that for 1988, Chevrolet revised the Corvette front suspension and changed the kingpin axis to a zero-scrub-radius design to aid yaw stability, especially effective at reducing brake pull when one wheel hits water or any other low-friction-coefficient surface. At the rear suspension, camber was reduced to allow the new 17-in. tires (now a 7-rib design vs last year's 5-rib tread for enhanced wet traction) to run flatter and increase stability while reducing camber steer.

Curiously enough, when we went back to our March 1986 test of that year's Corvette Z51, we found that the new car fared no better except in top speed. The extra 15 bhp, larger tires and wheels, higher capacity brakes and revised suspension of the 1988 Z51 seemed to give no edge on acceleration times, lateral gs or stopping distances. Still, the 1988 Z51 felt as good

or better than any stock Corvette of recent memory, and like they say, "a particular car on a particular track on any given day . . . ," the numbers were close. It may very well be that the current Z51 needs the royal treatment—370–400 bhp and 170–180-mph capability—to take advantage of the humongous tires and brakes. It's been rumored that the design specifications for the King of the Hill Vette include the ability to make 20 stops from 150 mph, one mile apart, with little or no fade. And these are the street brakes.

Of course, the object of testing the stock Z51 was to provide a baseline for the race cars, aka would-be Kings. Neither race car was what you would call fresh. Bakeracing No. 4's engine had two 6-hour races and a few hours of miscellaneous laps under its belt. Directly prior to the test, GM Mesa Proving Ground personnel slapped on a new set of steel composition head gaskets and hurriedly replaced the gearbox. The Morrison/Baker car came right off the trailer, with the Nelson Ledges 24-hour-enduro engine that ran so flawlessly.

As expected, launching 300-plus-horsepower Vettes for acceleration testing required some fancy clutch and throttle work to avoid smoking the tires or bogging on the line. But once the right combination was found, both cars reeled off 13-second, 100-plus-mph runs one after the other, the Baker car dipping into the low 13s. Excessive rear camber on the 360-bhp Morri-

Gazing into the (liquid) crystal ball

GIVEN THE SLIGHTEST excuse to test Chevrolet's legendary 2-seater, the *Road & Track* test department snaps shut its weekly reading of *Metalworking News* and hustles out the front door alternately tripping and stumbling under a load of 5th wheels, clipboards and dragging wires. It doesn't take much. Mistake a sneeze for C-o-r-VETTE and the east wing laces up its driving shoes; simple rumors at the water cooler can scramble the testing troops to full alert.

Sometimes it's the real thing. Fourteen times since mid-1983 we have strapped test equipment to Corvettes and gone for it. Here we tabulate the acceleration and terminal speeds from our metrological skirmishes involving production-pure Corvettes. With some give and take allowing for Continent-flung locations, plus varying degrees of afternoon heat or evening cool, the steady power improvements have had unmistakable effects.

However, along the way we've also sampled five horsepower over-achievers, Vettes with chips on their shoulders (improved ones in their control modules) and something to prove. Each bragged of between 300 and 400 bhp, a range that contains the 370–400 bhp predicted to lurk beneath the King of the Hill Vette's bonnet. Which led us to

some quick curve-fitting predictions.

Well, discounting the gear-limited top speed of the Morrison/Baker car (and giving credit to the very experienced right foot of Corvette's Jim Ingle helping the Twin Turbo's acceleration), we're going to go out on a limb and state that, when we lay our hands on it, a 370-

bhp King of the Hill Vette will rocket past 60 mph in 4.5 seconds, hit the quarter mile in 13.0 sec at 109 mph and ultimately touch 179 mph. Given 400 bhp, make those figures 4.3 sec, 12.5 sec at 113.0 mph, and 184 mph. Now that's Testarossa and Ruf Twin-Turbo territory. Or better. —*Kim Reynolds*

STANDARD CORVETTE TEST RESULTS

Test date	Bhp	0–60 mph, sec	¼ mile, sec @ mph	Top speed, mph
March 1983	205	7.1	15.5 @ 88.0	137
August 1983	205	7.0	15.3 @ 87.5	139
January 1984	205	7.1	15.6 @ 88.5	136
December 1984	230	6.6	15.0 @ 91.0	149
September 1985	230	5.5	14.8 @ 98.5	154
February 1986	230	5.8	14.4 @ 96.0	154
September 1986	230	6.1	14.7 @ 97.0	na
June 1987	240	6.3	14.8 @ 95.0	133
February 1988	245	6.0	14.6 @ 95.5	est 158

HOT CORVETTE TEST RESULTS

	Bhp	0–60 mph, sec	¼ mile, sec @ mph	Top speed, mph
Bakeracing Corvette	325	4.5	13.2 @ 107.0	169
Callaway Twin Turbo (R&T, October 1986)	345	5.0	13.7 @ 104.0	178
Morrison/Baker Corvette	360	4.9	13.7 @ 103.5	127[1]
Anesi Corvette (R&T, March 1985)	385	4.2	12.7 @ 108.5	172
Twin Turbo Corvette (R&T, September 1985)	400	4.3	12.2 @ 117.0	191

[1]Non-overdrive transmission.

68

... launching 300-plus-bhp Vettes for acceleration testing required some fancy clutch and throttle work ...

PERFORMANCE

	1988 Chevrolet Corvette Z51	Bakeracing SCCA Escort Corvette	Morrison/Baker Nelson Ledges Corvette
Acceleration:			
Time to distance, sec:			
0–100 ft	2.9	2.6	2.9
0–500 ft	8.0	7.2	7.4
0–900 ft	11.5	10.4	10.7
0–1320 ft (¼ mi)	14.6	13.2	13.7
Speed at end			
of ¼ mi, mph	95.5	107.0	103.5
Time to speed, sec:			
0–30 mph	1.8	1.4	1.7
0–40 mph	2.8	2.3	2.5
0–50 mph	4.3	3.3	3.6
0–60 mph	6.0	4.5	4.9
0–70 mph	7.8	5.8	6.4
0–80 mph	10.0	7.4	8.1
0–90 mph	12.8	9.2	10.2
0–100 mph	16.6	11.3	12.7
Top speed, mph[1]	est 158	169	127[2]
Firebird Raceway lap time,			
min:sec[3]	1:15.2	1:11.6	1:10.5
Fuel economy, mpg	17.5	10.0 (racing)	10.0 (racing)
Braking:			
Average decel from			
60 mph, g[4]	0.89	0.97	0.95
Equivalent distance from			
60 mph, ft	135	124	127
Overall brake rating	excellent	excellent	excellent
Handling:			
Lateral accel, g	0.89	1.04	0.99
Slalom speed, mph	64.4	68.6	65.3

[1]Aided by tailwind and slight downhill. [2]Non-overdrive 5-sp transmission (rpm limited). [3]See sidebar on track testing. [4]Obtained using g·analyst.

CALCULATED DATA

	1988 Chevrolet Corvette Z51	Bakeracing SCCA Escort Corvette	Morrison/Baker Nelson Ledges Corvette
Lb/bhp (test weight)	14.0	10.2	9.6
Bhp/liter	42.7	56.6	60.9
R&T steering index	0.79	0.79	0.95

Bakeracing No. 4 (left) was tops in acceleration, top speed, brake, slalom and skidpad testing, but the Morrison/Baker car (below) turned the best lap times.

ALL THE KING'S HORSES AND ALL THE KING'S MEN

son car hurt its ability to hook up off the line, and its siamesed intake runners, while good for optimal flow at high rpm, inhibited cylinder filling at low rpm.

Running the 5-mile high-banked GM circular track and exploring the limits of the top-speed envelope were opportunities both race teams looked forward to. First out was Bakeracing

> *Chevrolet . . . could be holding a royal flush.*

No. 4. On the 2nd lap, Baker's digital readout speedometer climbed to 165 mph, and stayed there, even as the car accelerated all the way to 169 mph, as recorded on our radar gun.

The Morrison/Baker car, with its non-overdrive 5-speed Nash transmission, was next. Set up for the relatively low-speed Nelson Ledges course, it topped out at 127 mph at 5400 rpm—right on the rev limiter. So much for King of the Hill-simulating top speed.

With the power portion of our test completed, it was time to give the Vettes' suspensions and brakes a workout. Here, the brake and tire sizes of the stock Z51 car and Morrison/Baker race car were identical, the shorter stopping distance and grippier (near 1g) lateral acceleration figures of the latter attributable to harder, metallic brakes and softer, shaved S-compound tires. But once again, the Baker No. 4 car, running last year's

Taking (showroom) stock of the situation

NOBODY KNOWS MORE about building and driving Corvettes for showroom stock than Bakeracing's Kim Baker. In addition, he's a previous 2-time National Autocross Champion. So when the opportunity arose during our Firebird testing (the track, not the car), we bundled Kim into all three Corvettes—stock 1988, 1987 Bakeracing Escort Vette and Morrison/Baker 1988 prototype—and asked him to share his thoughts with us on how each one performed:

Firebird lapping

Stock 1988 Z51 Corvette. This car cornered at higher slip angles than the two race cars, primarily because of the deeper tread on the unshaved tires. The car felt as I expected on nearly full-tread tires and was very easy to correct out of any situation. I deliberately threw the car sideways a few times to test recovery, and it proved to be easy to catch, with negligible loss of time.

The suspension was basically the same as that of the Morrison/Baker prototype, but without the bad feel to the steering or bottoming of the suspension. I would like to have tried this car with shaved 17-in. S-compound tires, as I believe that it would have outperformed the prototype on the skidpad and slalom course. With the engine, but not the gear ratios from the prototype, this car would have been very fast.

My only complaint about the suspension was that more shock damping was needed for the Phoenix track.

Bakeracing Escort Corvette. This car has a stock Z51 suspension and 16-in. S-compound Goodyears, coupled with

precise and optimized alignment settings designed for Sebring. Its Bilstein shocks were valved for Sebring, and the suspension was biased for right-hand turns. The engine is a 1987 model updated to 1988 specifications, assembled to the Escort Endurance Showroom Stock regulations and exactly as raced and inspected by SCCA after its Sebring enduro 1st-place finish.

On the track the engine had a very wide power band; the suspension felt comfortable—well-balanced and easiest to drive. I could hit the apexes easily. It was difficult getting traction on the straight where the drag strip starts, but I think that was due to the track conditions early in the day. I would like to try this car with 17-in. tires.

I feel the lap times for all three cars lacked validity, because there was no opportunity for controlled comparison testing and the earliest runs were the most slippery because the track was sandy and cool. Later on, conditions did improve but the track was still slower than usual. My subjective impressions, however, would still be valid.

Morrison/Baker 1988 prototype. The gearbox ratios were not well suited to the engine or differential gearing, and as a result, the engine's power curve could not be fully exploited.

After taking a few laps to become accustomed to the car on a race track, I found it was impossible to get the car well-balanced. If I braked into a corner, there was severe trailing-throttle oversteer. When I braked in a straight line and drove into the corner, the car would not turn in. Additionally, once into a steady-state cornering mode, the car

would push, understeering even more as the power was gradually applied, then suddenly changing to oversteer. It also felt as though the suspension was occasionally riding on the bump stops.

I could tell by the way the steering felt that there was a problem with the front-suspension geometry, possibly as simple as excessive positive caster. The steering had a nonlinear, somewhat notchy feel in both the slalom and on the road course. Perhaps the car is overtricked; it needs a different setup to take advantage of the very sticky 17-in. S-compound Goodyear tires.

Slalom

Stock 1988 Z51 Corvette. This car felt very good, except for the large slip angles generated by the full-tread tires. I had to turn-in slightly earlier than I had with the race cars—four wheels sliding, and good throttle response. I used 2nd gear, as the car wouldn't stick well enough for 3rd and the tires got a little slower toward the end of the runs.

Bakeracing No. 4. It was the easiest car to drive fast. I could almost go as fast as I could turn the wheel, but my slalom skills were too rusty to exploit the full potential of the car. No counter steering was necessary, there was very little sliding, 3rd gear worked best and the tires stayed consistent.

Morrison/Baker 1988 prototype. The steering felt odd. Third gear offered a perfect ratio for the slalom, but required a delicate balance of power to keep the rear end from sliding. I had to use the throttle to turn a fast time through the slalom, but the tires remained stable.

—*Kim Baker*

70

smaller 255/50ZR-16 tires and smaller 1987 rear brakes, out-cornered and outbraked the other two cars, pulling nearly 1g on deceleration and a healthy 1.04g lateral acceleration. Proving it's not so much the ingredients as it is the chef. In the capable hands of Kim Baker, 700-ft slalom speeds were some of the best we've ever tested. The Bakeracing No. 4 Vette traversed the cones at 68.6 mph, just 3.6 mph off the absolute record set by the Swift DB-1 Formula Ford in March 1984.

Numbers are numbers, but sometimes a car's performance is more than the sum of its parts. Such was the case with the Morrison car that, in individual tests, emerged an embarrassing 2nd to the Baker car every time. At Firebird Raceway's 1.5-mile road course, however, things were different. With Kim Baker and John Heinricy each getting 10 laps behind the wheel of every car, the Morrison/Baker Vette—nearly 5 sec quicker

than the stock Z51 and more than 1 sec quicker than Bakeracing No. 4—finally showed what it was made for—road racing.

All of which proves what? That a couple of sticky-tired, tweaked and tuned, 300-plus-horsepower Vette race cars can outrun the best production Z51 Vette Chevy can muster? You knew that already. But squint a bit. Imagine 370–400 horsepower bridled under the hood, wider-still rear wheels and tires and rear bodywork to keep all that rubber in-house, and one of the 10 best performance cars in the world today may just become a world beater tomorrow. Chevrolet—which in its best poker face says, "What King?"—could be holding a royal flush.

When, and you'll notice we didn't say if, Chevy lifts the bow-tie curtain of secrecy on the King of the Hill Corvette, we'll test one right here on these pages. And we're not just crowning around.

Gone Kingfishin'

AT 60 MPH, upshift into 2nd gear. The tach's liquid-crystal display should read 7200 rpm—redline. Then, as you merge into traffic, try to keep it below 7200 rpm as you run it up through the gears—all six of them. At 160 mph, shift into 6th gear. Sounds like a pit crew coaching a race car driver sorting out a new IMSA GTO ride. But actually, it could be a Chevy salesman giving a few driving tips to one of 5000 or so lucky buyers who just drove a 1989 King of the Hill Corvette off the showroom floor. That is, after plunking down a cool $50,000–$55,000.

Could this be the 400-bhp, aluminum-block, aluminum-head, 4-cam V-8 Corvette ZR1 that General Motors Vice President Lloyd Reuss announced at the Specialty Equipment Manufacturer's Association (SEMA) trade show in Las Vegas this past November? Could be and is. The long-awaited Super Vette (to be sold alongside your more garden-variety coupes and roadsters) should hit dealer showrooms this fall. And when it does, it will do its part to restore the image of a corporate giant that's been stuck in its own moat—in engineering leadership, in product innovation, in market share—for several years now.

Although one could scarcely tell from the outside (particularly the front), the King of the Hill Corvette marks the most significant overhaul of Chevrolet's 2-seater since the current generation's introduction in mid-1983—perhaps since the introduction of the first small-block V-8 in 1955. Because the hallowed Chevy small-block, centerpiece of the Vette and that division's performance image maker for more than three de

cades, is being tossed in favor of a new powerplant. Because although the displacement still says 350 cu in., this heart transplant is all-new, a cooperative venture with Lotus Engineering. It flies directly in the face of decades of staleness at GM, of creative strangulation and the dreaded not-invented-here syndrome.

To wit: aluminum-alloy block and heads; 4 chain-driven camshafts operating 32 valves; 16-runner tuned-port intake manifold, 8 long ones for good low-speed response and 8 short ones for

PHOTO BY JIM DUNNE/POPULAR MECHANICS

Somewhat shy King of the Hill 1989 prototype with convex rear-end cap, squarish taillamps and 400-bhp LT5.

Sideways-mounted Corvette Indy 350/32 has as many cams as most Chevys have cylinders; LT5 mounts longitudinally.

heavy high-rpm breathing; reverse-flow hybrid cooling system; water-cooled oil filter; a push-type pressure plate instead of the more conventional pull variety; 6-speed ZF transmission with two overdrive ratios. Got your attention yet? Needless to say, the added cams and intake runners make for a very full engine compartment. So crowded, in fact, that the dual catalytic converters mounted directly downstream of the exhaust manifolds (required to light off hydrocarbons to meet emission standards) force a relocation of the starter—to atop the engine, beneath the intake runners.

Sources claim a reliable 370 bhp and 350 lb-ft of torque at this time; whether Chevrolet releases a 400-bhp, 400 lb-ft King engine for this fall is unclear. Also in doubt (at least for the 1989 model year) is the ZF 6-speed, which may not be ready until 1990. GM needs that transmission with its extra tall top gear to get good highway EPA mileage ratings and keep the King out of the Gas Guzzler category. Though many enthusiasts would gladly pay the $500 or so fine (now levied on a bevy of Euro imports, from Aston Martin and BMW to Lamborghini and Volvo), GM's policy is to avoid that stigma.

Lest we forget: Getting the power to the ground will be a set of massive 315/35ZR-17 tires mounted on 11-in. "Cuisinart" wheels. And the rear-quarter panels will be widened 1½ in. each to accommodate the beefy skins. As for the big brakes, 275/40ZR-17 front tires and revised suspension geometry that's due in the King, you can buy those items right now in the 1988 Z51.

—Ron Sessions

TWIN-TURBO CORVETTE

Its 300 km/h top speed makes this Callaway special-order exotic the first US qualifier for the world's most exclusive car club. Hans-Jürgen Tücherer applies its 287 kW of blown firepower to the tarmac...

REEVES Callaway of Old Lyme, Connecticut has added a few logs to the already well-stoked "World's Fastest Car" fire. Not satisfied with the 286 km/h recorded in his 255 kW Callaway Corvette Twin Turbo in 1987 form, for '88 he has come up with a few more mind-expanding tricks.

"During 1987 we found that some detailed work would make our production car even faster and stronger," says the man who has already sold 200 examples of his twin-huffer, customised American sports car. The results speak for themselves. In 1988 form, the Callaway 'Vette has now become the first American production car (albeit very limited production) to break the 300 km/h barrier, and amid the picturesque autumnal hues of Connecticut we were given ample opportunity to test-drive the US-rocket for ourselves.

Optically, the new tuned Corvette is closer to the stock model than the '87 model. Gone are the NACA ducts on the bonnet and in their place is a complicated system to provide cold air to the highly polished intercoolers for the twin turbo system. The air is now drawn from intricate ducts in the nose, led through large tracts on the underside of the engine hood, on both sides of the engine, and fed directly to intercoolers.

"This is a very expensive solution but it has two exciting advantages," explains Callaway: "the aerodynamics are improved, thanks to the removal of the ducts on the hood, and this is very important for achieving maximum speed. Also, we are now getting more air to the intercoolers and that's very positive when it comes to making more horsepower."

Sticking to the air-waves for a moment, Reeves was also forced to devise a new system for feeding air to the fuel injection system, which is retained with the turbo installation. This involved using some of the chassis channels as air tracts. And then it was the turn of the engine management system to be massaged, Callaway's people developing their own microchip to re-programme fuel supply and ignition timing.

Microchip tuning

Hmm, lots of work and many hours on the dynamometer, but now let's talk about power. The good news is that there is now 287 kW produced at 4 250 r/min by the 5,7-litre small block Chevy V8. Oh, and we should mention that this increase comes with the help of two IHI turbochargers

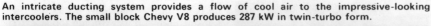

An intricate ducting system provides a flow of cool air to the impressive-looking intercoolers. The small block Chevy V8 produces 287 kW in twin-turbo form.

enlarged over last year's model. They dish up 60 kPa of boost and they also start working at low revs. You can feel that the claimed 780 N.m of torque at 2 750 r/min is no pipe dream, though in this case the smoke all comes from the 275 Goodyear Eagles fitted to the rear wheels.

With a perfect dose of throttle and clutch you can reach 100 km/h in 4,8 seconds from standstill and you can pulverise the quarter mile (400 m) in less than 13 seconds. American magazines tested the car to a maximum speed of 303 km/h and that means that at last, in the form of the

The Callaway Corvette looks very close to a stock model (above), the special rims and tyres being a major distinguishing factor. But if Callaway are trying to win sales from Porsche's 928 S4 in Europe, they will have to soften the rather gaudy interior (below).

Callaway Corvette, an American car can be admitted to the exclusive 300-club.

Driving the car

Everything works easily: the boosted small-block starts building power from low speeds and the Doug Nash gearbox must be shifted with some effort, but is very precise. Also, there is the advantage of overdrive. With a push of a button you get three extra speeds on the upper three gears, so you can play with seven speeds to guarantee you lots of fun, or you can simply select overdrive fourth and luxuriate in all that torque.

In the handling department, Callaway supply the optional Z-51 chassis package which gives an even firmer ride and goes well with the 9,5J X 17 aluminium wheels, developed by Callaway in conjunction with the English company, Dymag. The Goodyear Eagles in 275/40 ZR 17 size harmonise nicely with the sports chassis and happily for peace of mind, are rated to the speeds that we are talking of here.

The only point for discomfort is the imprecise power steering, which doesn't give you much in the way of road feel. But the brakes have outstanding qualities: the anti-lock system provided can also be fitted with bigger discs and calipers to prevent fading problems.

Unfortunately we couldn't drive up to real top-speed potential in Connecticut because the police are very strict

To cope with 300 km/h speeds, Z-rated Goodyear Eagles are fitted to Callaway's special wheels. The wide rubber adds aggression to the rear-end styling treatment (below).

and even the useful Passport radar detector is no guarantee against a stop-off in the local jail if you happen to flash past the Sheriff at 280-plus.

Still, it was enough to convince us that with the Callaway car you now have a real competitor for the Zuffenhausen bullet, in other words the Porsche 928 S4, even though they represent two totally different technological ideologies. Nearly everywhere, the Corvette is faster than the Porsche, and if Chevrolet could change some details in the interior, Reeves Callaway would surely sell a good chunk of the 400 cars he has scheduled for production this year, outside of America. A baby-blue interior is unlikely to find many friends on the eastern side of the Atlantic and some high class leather here, some wood there would

make the Corvette a real eye-catcher.

Apart from the Porsche 959, the Callaway Corvette is the only member of the 300-club to be fitted with a catalytic converter. And in the US the price is not too shocking by our standards. Over and above the 32 000 US dollars it costs you for a basic Corvette, you will have to take a bond for a further 26 000, not to mention shipping costs and import duties which could more than double the bill in South Africa. And for a little more, you can also have a turbocharged Corvette convertible. Open heaven for you?

The world's fastest?

In a recent shoot-out with some highly modified exotica – a Ruf Porsche twin-turbo, a Mercedes AMG Hammer and the odd Ferrari Testarossa – Callaway's experimental twin-turbo car, on which Reeves tries out all his more outlandish fantasies, took the unofficial title of the World's Fastest Street Car, when it ran to a timed 358 km/h (with a best one-way run of 370) at the Transportation Research Centre in mid-Ohio, on a 12 km banked oval track. This very special Corvette features lots more boost, bigger turbos and a claimed 530 kW at 6 750 r/min. Yet it is street legal, although road testers report that it needs lots of coaxing to avoid plug fouling and ''shuddered disconcertingly'' at low speed. We could forgive it for that, we think... ●

Ace of Clubs

Now here's a pair to draw to:
Porsche 911 Club Sport versus Chevrolet Corvette Z51.

BY RICH CEPPOS

• The newest version of the Porsche 911 spells out its mission in crisp letters along the inboard side of its left front fender. From the driver's seat you can take in the large, stylized "CS" logo and the words "Club Sport" at a glance, a message that's all the more seductive because it's hidden from other drivers by the soft curve of the 911's headlight sheetmetal.

Club Sport. It's a name that conjures up images of club racing, motorsport in general, the rigors of competition—and the glory of victory. Porsche has covered itself in racing glory, but it is not known for festooning front fenders with hype.

So what is this new fender inscription all about? "Porsche clubs all over the world hold competitive driving events at their meets," explains Jim Ryan, executive V.P. of sales and marketing for Porsche Cars

North America. "The Club Sport evolved from that, because it's where a lightened version would be more competitive."

The Club Sport, then, is a stripped-down, toned-up version of the aged but ageless 911, squeezed for yet another increment of speed and handling. Porsche expects it to be taken to the track and has revised it in several ways to improve its performance there. Still, says Ryan, the Club Sport package stops far short of the Porsche 934 IMSA racer of the mid-seventies. "Oh, it's not like that at all. The Club Sport had to retain full streetability."

More on that later. What's most important right now is that the Zuffenhausen works has mailed a leaned-on 911 to this country, wearing a fender decal that boasts, "I'm a bad-ass, come and get me."

Sounds to us like a high-noon challenge

to the home-town gunslinger. The one wearing the famous bow tie.

So say hello again to the club-sport version of the Chevrolet Corvette, better known as the Z51. This car also has a reputation to uphold. During the three seasons it competed in the SCCA's Showroom Stock endurance series, it never lost a race—and in the process it gunned down the quickest 944 Turbos that the Porsche factory could muster.

"The Z51 is as close to a competition setup for the Corvette as we can go, while still having the car be livable on the street," says John Heinricy, the product-engineering manager for the Corvette and the Camaro. Heinricy, a winning Showroom Stock Corvette racer himself, tuned the Z51's suspension on the race-track. "The Z51 is the ultimate in perfor-

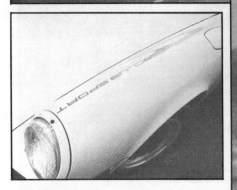

mance,'' he says. ''It is not something we want for our high-volume model.''

It's apparent that both the Z51 and the Club Sport come to this showdown with something to prove. Both are legendary grand-touring automobiles pushed as far in the race-car direction as their makers dared to push them. They are, in short, two tough hombres. And no matter which quick-draw artist owns your loyalties, you know that when these two meet, you're going to see one hell of a shoot-'em-up.

Which brings us to the question of the hour: Who sells the hottest club-sport machine you can buy? Which company builds the Ace of Clubs?

To determine the answer, we challenged one 911 Club Sport and one Vette Z51 to face each other in four duels: our standard battery of performance tests, an autocross course, a lapping session on a road-racing circuit, and a two-day flog over some of Southern California's most spectacular drivers' roads.

We've run similar tests before, but crowning the Ace of Clubs required a shift of emphasis. In most of our comparisons, a car's track performance is secondary to its over-the-road comportment. But the Club Sport and the Z51 are designed specially for extracurricular thrill rides. Their performance envelopes are so large, they require extra postage. Because both cars are supposed to be heroes on the track as well as on the road, we'll give equal weight

to each of our four contests.

Before the shooting begins, however, let's take a close look at what sets these rivals apart from their respective bunkmates. The Porsche 911 Club Sport's story can be summed up as ''less is more.'' Over the years the 911 has become increasingly luxurious; but luxuries add weight, and weight is the enemy of speed. The Club Sport is the Weight Watchers 911. For a base price of $45,895—the same amount you pay for a fully equipped Carrera—you get a car *without* the following items: A/C, a stereo, power windows and locks, sound-deadening insulation, rear jump seats, armrests, and a passenger's-side sun visor. The benefit of self-denial is a saving of 155 pounds, according to Porsche.

And this diet comes with dessert: a helping of sporting stuff to spice up the 911's performance. A chin spoiler and the famous Porsche whale tail increase downforce and improve high-speed stability. Stiffer sport shocks tighten wheel control. The 214-hp, 3.2-liter, all-alumi-

num flat six gets hollow intake valves and a new chip for its control computer to raise the rpm cutoff from 6520 to 6840. A shortened, quick-throw shifter allows faster gear changes. Deeply winged sport seats bear-hug you in the turns. Our test car wore optional, extralarge Dunlop SP Sport D40s, size 205/55VR-16 up front and 225/50VR-16 in the rear. The only tasty bit conspicuous by its absence was an anti-lock braking system, which is not available on any 911.

Next to Porsche's lean, mean new kid in town, the Z51 Vette seems relaxed and friendly—perhaps too friendly for its own good. There is neither strain nor pain in the way it delivers its performance. Every standard Corvette comfort feature is present: air conditioning; a stereo; cruise control; tilt-telescope steering; power windows, mirrors, and locks; and a removable roof panel. And, yes, it has armrests and a full set of sun visors.

Ordering the Z51 package, however, triggers an important sequence of events as your car moves down the assembly line.

The frame gets special reinforcements (shared with the Z52 street-suspension package). A version of the fuel-injected, 5.7-liter V-8 delivering 245 hp—that's 5 hp more than the base Corvette enjoys—drops into the engine bay. The cooling system gets an oil cooler, a power-steering cooler, and a pair of pusher fans in front of the radiator. Every Z51 is equipped with a special version of the computer-controlled four-speed-plus-overdrive manual gearbox, including a shorter, 0.68:1 overdrive ratio. The final-drive ratio is 3.07:1, the shortest in the Corvette parts bin.

The Z51 chassis pieces include stiffer springs and suspension bushings, larger anti-roll bars, Bilstein gas shocks with tighter valving, and a quick-ratio steering gear. Like all Vettes, the Z51 gets Bosch anti-lock brakes, but the standard twelve-inch front rotors give way to new, thirteen-inch discs, the largest in Corvette history. For maximum adhesion, 275/40ZR-17 Goodyear Eagle ZR40 tires on 9.5-inch-wide alloy wheels steamroller the pavement.

Now that you know the dimensions of this disagreement, it's time to find out whether the local hero from Warren, Michigan, can outdraw the wily newcomer from Zuffenhausen, West Germany. Yankee ingenuity or German engineering? On to the first showdown.

The Test Track

As you can see from the *C/D* Test Results box, the 911 once again demonstrated that a superior power-to-weight ratio wins the drag race every time. The 911 showed its whale tail to the Vette in the 0-to-60-mph sprint, beating the Chevy 5.6 seconds to 6.0. It remained ahead at the quarter-mile stripe, posting a 13.9-second elapsed time at 99 mph, versus the Vette's 14.2-second, 98-mph run. Only at the top end did the Vette pull ahead, reaching 152 mph—5 mph faster than the 911.

The 911 Club Sport surprised us in one respect, however: it was no quicker and no faster than the fully equipped, 200-hp Carrera we tested in 1984. For this we have no explanation. Nor does Porsche.

The 911 went on to nip the Vette in the slalom run—another surprise, considering the Z51's viselike, 0.89-g grip on the asphalt. (The Porsche held on until 0.85 g.) For the record, we achieved these roadholding figures on a new, extra-sticky skidpad, and we suspect that both are a touch higher than we would have recorded on our regular surface.

The Vette countered the Porsche's slalom victory with a 172-foot stop from 70 mph, 15 feet shorter than the 911 could manage. By the time we completed our first round of performance events, neither car could claim the lead.

The Autocross

There is not much point in buying either of these hot rods if you don't drop in

for at least a few of your local SCCA chapter's autocrosses. For test purposes we set up our own tricky combination of twists, turns, and abbreviated straights. Our course required no gear higher than second and took just under a minute to thread through.

Whether you're talking Corvette Z51 or 911 Club Sport, fun is never in question on an autocross course. Both cars offer enough sheer power, grip, and braking ability to entertain the most jaded competitors.

The way our two test cars went about their work, however, was as different as their color schemes. The 911 will teach your right foot a new way of living. Twenty-three years of development has removed some of the quirkiness from Son of Beetle's handling but hasn't tamed it entirely. The 911 demands that you do virtually all of your braking in a straight line or run the risk of entering a turn with the rear end slewing. Jerk your foot off the throttle in the middle of a corner and the tail-heavy 911 begins to pirouette. Mash your foot back down and it switches abruptly to heavy understeer.

The secret to getting through the orange cones quickly in a 911 *and* having a good time is to play its throttle the way Isaac Stern plays his violin: you caress it, you coax it, you squeeze it gently. No fiddling allowed. Blend in smooth steering motions and the 911 digs neatly into the turns, sliding its front or rear end as you see fit.

The Z51, in contrast, is what computer types would call user-friendly. Yank the wheel 90 degrees off center and the Vette will practically knock the wind out of you as it rams your shoulder into the door. Yet it's so naturally coordinated it will make a rank novice think he's a budding Alain

Prost. Compared with the 911, the Z51 responds like an F-16.

In an autocross, the Vette acts like your best drinking buddy, as if it knows just what you're thinking. It responds to your orders with "Hey, no sweat" confidence. The steering points with authority, and the ABS takes the worry out of late braking. You have to do something truly weird to spin out in this car.

If autocrossing were a contest of fun alone, we'd have another draw on our hands. But it's not. Speed counts, too, and on that score the Vette is the clear winner, posting a 53.1-second time through our course, versus the 911's 54.3.

The Racetrack

Now we raise the ante. Both Porsche and Chevrolet figure their club-sport models will see high-speed duty on road-racing circuits, so we put both cars to the test on one. Our venue was Willow

		price, base/as tested	engine	SAE net power/torque	transmission/ gear ratios:1/ axle ratio:1	curb weig lb
Vital Statistics	CHEVROLET CORVETTE Z51	$29,480/$32,420	V-8, 350 cu in (5733cc), iron block and aluminum heads, GM electronic engine-control system with port fuel injection	245 bhp @ 4300 rpm/ 340 lb-ft @ 3200 rpm	4-speed with electronic overdrive/ 2.88, 1.91, 1.34, 1.00; 0.68/ 3.07	3320
	PORSCHE 911 CLUB SPORT	$45,895/$47,561	SOHC flat 6, 193 cu in (3164cc), aluminum block and heads, Bosch Motronic engine-control system with port fuel injection	214 bhp @ 5900 rpm/ 195 lb-ft @ 4800 rpm	5-speed/ 3.50, 2.06, 1.41, 1.13, 0.89/ 3.44	2700

		acceleration, sec						top speed, mph	braking, 70–0 mph, ft	roadholdin 300-ft skidpa
		0–30 mph	0–60 mph	0–100 mph	¼-mile	top gear, 30–50 mph	top gear, 50–70 mph			
Car and Driver Test Results	CHEVROLET CORVETTE Z51	2.1	6.0	14.7	14.2 @ 98 mph	5.0	5.0	152	172	0.89
	PORSCHE 911 CLUB SPORT	1.9	5.6	14.1	13.9 @ 99 mph	8.0	8.7	147	187	0.85

diabolical Turn Nine, a high-speed, fourth-gear swoop, the Club Sport turned downright ornery, twitching its tail and sidestepping like a cabaret dancer. It was enough to make us back off.

Which is how the Vette blew the paint off the 911 on the racetrack. The Porsche's best lap time was 1 minute 44.2 seconds. The Vette zipped around in just 1:41.0.

The Road

Because the Club Sport and the Z51 are both street cars at heart, it's logical to assume that most of their lucky owners will get at least some of their driving jollies from taming long stretches of unruly two-lane. So just how good are these cars in the real world?

We based our assessment of their over-the-road capabilities on two days of varied driving, with extra emphasis on their behavior on challenging mountain roads. We conducted our canyon blasts on two of California's most memorable byways: the Angeles Forest Highway (N3) and the Angeles Crest Highway (California 2), forming a route that shakes, rattles, and rolls from Palmdale to Pasadena. Both roads cling to ridges and mountainsides in the Angeles National Forest and are blessed with countless switchbacks, devilish changes in elevation, and breathtaking drop-offs. Rapid progress requires precise technique—and confidence in your equipment.

The Porsche closed the gap in our mountain-road runoff. Our racetrack experience with the 911 made us careful to burn off all excess speed before entering a turn. Driven according to the in-slow, out-fast philosophy, the 911 was agile, communicated well, and felt safe. No tail fakes, no untoward moves. Its unassisted steer-

CONTINUED ON PAGE 84

Springs International Raceway, a gut-tightening, 2.5-mile serpent that climbs the side of a foothill in the Mojave Desert. High velocity is what Willow is all about: our speeds down the front and back straights exceeded 120 mph, and we took five of Willow's nine turns in either fourth or fifth gear.

The balance of power between the Cor-vette and the Porsche tilted dramatically at Willow. The plastic Chevy remained stable and unflappable through the track's white-knuckle sweepers, while the 911 was nervous and unsure. Its tail felt like the heavy end of a pendulum; we found ourselves avoiding braking in the turns at all costs, lest the 911 launch into a series of eye-widening feints and darts. In Willow's

weight distribution, % F/R	dimensions, in				fuel tank, gal	suspension		brakes, F/R	tires
	wheelbase	length	width	height		front	rear		
51.2/48.8	96.2	176.5	71.0	46.7	20.0	ind, unequal-length control arms, plastic leaf spring, anti-roll bar	ind; fixed-length half-shaft, 2 lateral links, and 2 trailing links per side; plastic leaf spring; anti-roll bar	vented disc/ vented disc	Goodyear Eagle ZR40, P275/40ZR-17
40.7/59.3	89.5	168.9	65.0	52.0	22.5	ind, strut located by a control arm, torsion bars, anti-roll bar	ind, semi-trailing arms, torsion bars, anti-roll bar	vented disc/ vented disc	Dunlop SP Sport D40, F: 205/55VR-16; R: 225/50VR-16

maneuverability, 1000-ft slalom, mph	interior sound level, dBA				fuel economy, mpg			autocross course, sec	racecourse, min:sec
	idle	full throttle	70-mph cruising	70-mph coasting	EPA city	EPA highway	C/D observed		
64.3	56	82	76	74	17	24	12	53.1	1:41.0
65.9	59	86	78	76	18	25	15	54.3	1:44.2

FLAGSHIP ZR1

A CORVETTE THAT SETS A WORLD TECHNOLOGY STANDARD

By Ron Grable

Picture this: It's your favorite restaurant, you're with your favorite date, and you glide up to the valet in your new ZR1 Corvette. It's identified only by a subtle badge on the rear, but this teenage valet is hip—a car junkie—and he *knows* what it is. He's so anxious to get behind the steering wheel, he completely forgets about opening the door for your girlfriend, and hovers by your door instead, waiting to jump into the driver's seat. You tell your concerned date it's okay for the kid to park it (or whatever else he'll do), because

you've engaged the "valet" function, and the poor guy will only be able to get reduced power from the engine.

The heart of the new ZR1 Corvette clearly beats under the hood. Sure, there's other leading-edge technology aboard, but it's mostly there to accommodate the LT5 motor. The six-speed manual, monster tires and the dual-mass flywheel just wouldn't be necessary except to handle the power and torque coming off the end of the crankshaft. And it comes off in prodigious amounts. How does 300 ft.-lbs. of torque at 1000 rpm sound?

This engine was the outgrowth of a number of programs, which took place during the early Eighties in the Corvette engineering group, ostensibly to determine power levels and engine configurations for future-generation Vettes. There was a twin-turbo V8 program, where it was easy to establish almost any power level desired (a couple of turns of the boost screw), in which a total of 12 cars were built for evaluating driveline and handling. Another program involved a normally aspirated 350-cubic-inch V8 with 600 hp, so engi-

Photography: Bob D'Olivo, Petersen Photographic

Born on the drawing boards of Lotus Engineering and built to General Motors specs, the 5.7-liter LT5 engine is a blending of the talents of GM and Lotus engineers.

Engine sensors anticipate driver needs via throttle pressure, engine speed and manifold pressure, making several computer-controlled performance levels available. A key-activated "valet" switch keeps the engine in the lower performance mode when desired.

Could this be the ultimate Corvette? The new ZR1 is designed specifically to be the best-performing sports car in the world.

Two square exhaust pipes peek out of each indentation in the bumper. A subtle LT5 badge brands the Corvette as a ZR1.

neers could see what would be required of the chassis and brakes at prolonged high speeds. In addition, Chevrolet used Showroom Stock endurance racing to explore the durability and absolute strength limits of individual parts. The large Repco brakes found on current models are one example of higher-capacity parts that were a direct result of that racing program.

In addition to establishing the power levels for the future Vette, these programs allowed the engineers to identify some definite no-no's. They realized the engine for the new Vette would have to be a V8. (This was important enough that Corvette chief Dave McLellan said they would have stretched the wheelbase, if necessary, to accommodate one.) Only a

V8 would be acceptable from a smoothness and tractability standpoint, and data from the turbocharging programs told them it would have to be normally aspirated. Turbocharged fuel efficiencies and emissions fell short of the goal GM set for the Corvette, in respect to the gas-guzzler issue. Equally important, it was decided that turbocharging did not represent the "world technology" management wanted for the corporate flagship.

To capture this world-technology image, outside design firms were contacted and asked to bring their proposals to Chevrolet for an engine project. At this point, Chevrolet was comfortable with the chassis' ability to handle almost anything conceivable from a production motor. What

Visual changes in the '89 ZR1 include a softer, rounded look and cross-hatching on the square taillights.

they were looking for from the engine was a quantum leap in performance; they wanted an engine that would stretch the production-car performance potential to the limit.

In the early thinking stages, no power targets were established. Chevrolet wanted an engine that would push current technological boundaries, one that would lead the way for other manufacturers. In short, an engine worthy of occupying the space between the Vette frame rails. After all, there have been some great engines in there. In spring 1985, Tony Rudd of Lotus proposed an engine that seemed capable of meeting all the requirements. GM approved, and the LT5 was born on the drawing boards of Lotus Engineering.

With current technology, an engine displacing 5.7 liters easily produces 400 hp at 6000 rpm. The real challenges come in producing that sort of power level reliably, while maintaining practical numbers for everyday use. Lotus engineers were given some demanding parameters by Chevy engineering chief Fred Schaafsma. First, this was to be unequivocally the best-performing production car in the world. Second, the tractability must be at *least* the equal of the current car; ditto fuel economy, and finally, the engine had to fit in the existing car. (This created a

problem on the assembly line, as the engine is mated to the vehicle from the bottom up, through the frame rails. This meant the new engine could be no wider than the old.)

One important point made frequently by GM is that this is not a Lotus engine. It was a joint effort, with the specifications coming from powertrain chief engineer for V8 passenger cars Roy Midgley, the man responsible for making sure the finished product met all Chevrolet's re-

quirements. We can imagine the problems that must have surfaced during the project—besides the language barrier and the Atlantic Ocean. The fact that the engine is now a reality, that both sides are still talking to each other, and that the performance is everything expected, speaks well of the cooperation on both sides.

Producing 400 hp from 5.7 liters isn't difficult; everything else being in place, just use a large enough throttle to flow the correct amount of air. Do that, though, and the engine

probably wouldn't run at 1000 rpm. At low throttle settings and engine speeds, the air velocity through the large throttle would be slow and difficult to modulate. To meet Schaafsma's tractability goal, an innovative intake system was designed, incorporating the best of both worlds (large throttle for maximum power and small throttle for low speed control). This airflow system is the cornerstone of the engine, and is responsible for the extremely wide power band. Three airflow sensors (with individual throttle plates) feed into a cast-aluminum plenum, where 16 individual intake runners deliver the fuel/air mix to the cylinders, one runner for each intake valve. In the secondary runner for each cylinder, a throttle valve is fitted, controlled by the engine computer. All 16 runners have an individual fuel injector nozzle, also answering to the engine computer.

Three airflow sensors (one small, about the size of a quarter, the other two elliptical, approximately the area of a coffee cup) and the Electronic Control Module (ECM) manage the amount of air supplied to the engine. In low-demand situations, all the air is supplied by the small throttle plate; the other two remain closed. Using just this small throttle, the engine produces close to 30 hp (good for 90 mph). With such a small diameter, large changes in throttle angle have a small effect on total flow area, so manifold pressure excursions are minimized, with the desired high degree of throttle response and sensitivity. In this configuration, we have a large engine breathing through a small throttle. This is ideal for clean, sharp throttle response and good torque, because of the high air-inflow velocity.

As demand increases, the system clicks into stage two, where the two elliptical throttle plates open. As long as the engine speed stays below 3500 rpm, the computer keeps the butterflies in the secondary intake ports closed and their injectors off. Using all three throttle plates, the engine produces almost the same power as the current L-98 V8 (245 hp). (Incidentally, this configuration is what the valet gets to drive, thanks to a key-activated switch.)

Now for the serious stuff. When the computer sees full throttle, engine speed above 3500 rpm and a falling manifold pressure, it knows it's time to quit fooling around. The man up there needs it all. The driver's doing all he can with all three throttle plates open, so the computer bangs open the secondary intake butterflies and brings those eight injectors on line. Now it's all happening; the engine is using all 16 intake valves and all 16 injectors, spinning over 7000 rpm and producing almost 400 hp. Since these secondary ports and injectors only function at high power demand, they are sized accordingly, being slightly bigger than the primary ports. In addition, the cam lobes for the secondary valves have 20 degrees more duration than the primary lobes for more high-speed power.

The engineers had some concern about the effect of the secondary port when its butterfly was closed. Even though the butterfly remains shut, the valve continues to open and close. The engineers wanted to know what effect, if any, there would be on turbulence and mixing in the combustion chamber. At this point in the development cycle of the engine, no discernible effect has been noticed, but according to the project people, more work in this area may be necessary.

Previously, the airflow sensors on Vettes used the mass airflow system of measurement. This new LT5 intake uses speed-density measurement where the computer takes the data for manifold pressure, rpm, temperature and throttle position. Based upon an algorithm table, the

computer can "look up" the correct fuel/air ratio. Chevrolet chose the new method for reduced flow restrictions, but additional advantages include its simplicity and reliability.

General Manager of Lotus Engineering Ian Doble feels that no matter how sophisticated the intake system is, power and efficiency goals won't be met without the correct combustion chamber configuration. Combustion stability and speed are critical, so the components are arranged to promote good mixing and turbulence in the chamber. Inflow from the intake valves and the squish properties of the piston and cylinder head combine to achieve this, and the centrally located spark plug reduces the distance the flame front must travel to complete combustion. Heat is quickly removed from the surrounding area by the highly conductive aluminum and the close proximity of water passages. The extremely high 11.25:1 compression ratio is indicative of the efficiency of this combustion chamber. In addition, the engine will accommodate lower octane fuels, even as low as 90.

A narrow, 22-degree included angle for the valves and small-diameter drive gear for the DOHC cylinder heads helped keep the width of the engine down so it would fit through the existing frame rails. Included in the head design is a provision for oil to drain back into the sump during hard cornering, a welcome addition for a vehicle designed to produce over 1.2g cornering power.

The block is cast-aluminum with forged aluminum liners with Nikasil coating. This method should prove reliable in view of Porsche's success with the process. The block is split at the crank centerline, where an aluminum girdle, with cast-in-place nodular iron main bearing caps, is bolted in place. The girdle is held with no fewer than 28 bolts (two per each main bearing cap), which forms a rigid support for the crank and stabilizes the lower block area. The oil pickup is cast integrally with the aluminum sump, and a sheetmetal windage tray is used to control oil slosh, no mean feat in a vehicle with this cornering ability! Additional development is still underway in the area of oil slosh, as the engineers are not completely satisfied with the present setup.

The crankshaft and connecting rods are forged steel. The oil pump is driven from the front of the crank, and the ignition timing is taken from the crank center to eliminate torsional inaccuracies. Crank journals are

70 mm larger than those on the L-98 crankshaft, to deal with the additional power.

The LT5 uses four ignition coils, each handling two cylinders and firing every revolution of the crank, controlled by an expanded version ECM (static timing is no longer adjustable). The new ECM allows a more accurate match of fuel and spark requirements, and with the correct calibration in the module, a non-linear relationship is possible between fuel, throttle and rpm. The result of the new-generation ECM is more flexibility in calibrating horsepower and economy. The timing ring on the crank center also establishes timing for the sequential fuel injection. As many elements as possible were located in the engine V underneath the intake plenum: starter, ignition coils, air-conditioning compressor and alternator. The compressor, alternator, power steering pump and

Stopping power matches the awesome speed potential of the ZR1. The Repco brake system, with its larger-diameter brake rotors and stiffer dual-piston calipers, is a direct development of Chevrolet's Showroom Stock racing program.

The digital/bar instrument cluster is just as high tech as ever. Look for some impressive readouts from the new ZR1!

water pump are all driven by a single serpentine belt.

Also new for this engine is the manufacturing location—Mercury Marine in Stillwater, Oklahoma. MM has been associated with GM for years in converting automotive engines for marine use, and leads the industry in aluminum casting production and machining. The anticipated production volumes for this engine (initial rates of 18 per day with total capability of 50 per day) are in line with MMs experience. MM will dedicate a portion of its Stillwater plant to LT5 assembly, establishing a "clean-room" environment for the purpose. Each engine will be run on a "wet" dyno (running under power with fuel). Most engine assembly lines only turn the finished engines from an external power source to check for component leaks and other possible problems.

There's a rumor circulating to the effect that a nickel, placed on edge on an LT5 plenum, will remain there while the engine is cycled on the dyno between idle and 6000 rpm. Sounds a little too good to be true, but it's a fact that special attention is given to balance for this engine. All

reciprocating parts are assembled in matched sets, and the final balance spec is tight at 0.5 in.-oz. A critical customer will probably just be able to notice a 1.5-in.-oz. imbalance.

Standard equipment with the ZR1 option is the ZF six-speed manual transmission. To handle the increased torque output of the LT5, the distance between the input and output shafts was increased by 12 mm over the L-98 four-speed manual. One unfavorable result of this was an increased clunking and clattering (increased gear backlash) when torque reversals occurred, so the engineers came up with a dual-mass flywheel. Functionally, one flywheel mass is attached to the crankshaft and one to the transmission, with a viscous coupling between. This set-

up should effectively preload the gear sets to eliminate back lash.

Included in the transmission shifter assemblies are "blocker" solenoids, which can alter gear selection. If the computer sees the 1-2 shift begin when vehicle speed is between 12 to 20 mph and throttle position is less than 25 percent, it blocks second gear and allows the transmission to engage fourth instead. With the torque available at low rpm, it probably won't have much effect on ac-

All controls are comfortably placed in the Corvette cockpit, both on the dash and center console. The driver-determined ride control switch is located on the console, just behind the shifter.

celeration, and the window in which the computer intervenes is a low-demand situation anyway. It certainly smacks of Big Brotherism, but it was done to boost EPA figures and help avoid gas-guzzler fines.

Chevrolet can point to the Repco brake system on the ZR1 as a direct development of its Showroom Stock racing program. When the Corvette first entered SS endurance racing in 1985, its brakes were woefully inadequate. Year-by-year development has upgraded the brakes and wheels to the point where they are now capable of dealing with the awesome speed potential of the ZR1. The 17-inch wheels allow larger-diameter (read: capacity) brake rotors and stiffer dual piston calipers (front only), while the Goodyears are responsible for some impressive handling performance. The current Z51 option 13-inch front and 12-inch rear rotors will be used on the ZR1.

Visually, the only differences are in the rear, where the ZR1 has a softer, more rounded look, horizontal marks across the square taillights, four square exhaust pipes peeking out of the indentation in the bumper and, of course, the subtle LT5 badge.

The customer willing to cough up the extra money for the killer motor (we don't know how much extra yet), will be content in the knowledge that it is the most sophisticated, fastest, best-handling production car available in the world today. It doesn't have the visual impact of a Countach or Testarossa, but it should blow them both into the weeds without even raising its oil temperature.□

CONTINUED FROM PAGE 79

ing was an upper-body workout but was pleasantly direct. Its brakes were sure. Treated with respect, the 911 never bit.

Once again, though, the Vette proved the more inspiring. It was almost insensitive to slip-ups in technique and seemed to have limitless grip. Knowing ABS was there to back us up was worth an extra 5 mph into every corner. Not only was the Vette easier than the Porsche to drive quickly, but its power steering and air conditioning made it more comfortable. Advantage, Z51.

The Checkered Flag

We have arrived at the moment of truth, and truth does not favor the 911 Club Sport. Don't misunderstand: this Porsche is a delightful automobile, the nicest 911 we've ever driven. It has a sweet, mechanical disposition and a rev-me-forever engine. Its exhaust note is an exotic cross between the world's largest Hoover and a Group C race car. But when you reach for the air conditioner, it's not there. When you want some music, it's not there. When you want to pop open the sunroof, it's not there. The Club Sport is an interesting experiment, but it pales under the harsh light of common sense. Its performance advantage over a standard 911 Carrera is anything but clear, so what's the point? Only an inside-out Porsche nutball would pony up the price of a Carrera for a 911 lacking major comfort items. That may explain why Porsche Cars North America has imported only twenty 911 Club Sports for sale.

We are left with the winner: the car that turned in the big numbers and handled the high pressure with maximum class. We hereby proclaim the Chevrolet Corvette Z51 the Ace of Clubs.

The trophy comes with a warning label, however: Beware of the ride. The Z51 will get by just fine in the Sunbelt states, where the roads are smooth as desktops. But our experience with Z51s in Michigan suggest that this car will pound your brain to mush on the winter-worn highways of the northern climes. (We suspect the 911 Club Sport wouldn't be much better.)

And to those of you in the Corvette cheering section who are rushing to your typewriters to point out that the Club Sport costs half again as much as the Z51, consider this: the 911's fit, finish, and solidity are so far superior to the Corvette's that the price difference seems justified on that score alone.

But enough nit-picking. We came looking for rawboned gunslingers, and we found them. And now we have a winner. Kindly tip your Stetsons in the direction of Warren, Michigan, where the big gun in club sports sits with its back to the garage wall, waiting. ●

It's an object lesson in the Doppler effect. In the overcast dawn of an Ohio morning, the Corvette comes out of the corner as a small red dot, barely visible to the naked eye. Within seconds it hurtles down the straight, the intensity of its big-inch small-block growing even louder. As it approaches, the pitch of the maxed-out motor changes—

waaaaaaaaaaAAAAAAAAAooooooooooow!!!

—and in the instant of maximum intensity the red 'Vette flashes by on its way to the timers at the end of the straight. As we watch the 'Vette disappear into the haze, a voice breaks the silence over the radio:

"First Pass: One Seven Six Point Nine Five Miles Per Hour."

At first there is celebration in the pits. Then someone notes, "He won't be happy with that." The assumption is correct as

WHAT'S IT TAKE TO RUN 184 MPH, 12-SECOND E.T.'s, AND 30 MPG? JUST A LITTLE JOHN LINGENFELTER ENGINE MAGIC

By Jeff Smith

MAXIMUM OVERDRIVE

John Lingenfelter greets the news with a thinly disguised frown: "It should do better than that."

That's when it started to rain . . . .

DAY ONE

John Lingenfelter had called two months before: "Would you be interested in an '86 street-driven Corvette that could run 12-second e.t.'s, get 30 miles per gallon, and do 170 mph, all on street tires?" A few weeks later, I was standing in John's shop looking at what appeared to be a stock '86 Corvette.

"Dyno" Bob Vanderhart was busily bolting on a set of Lingenfelter's new larger runners to the Tuned Port manifold. Not surprisingly, the small-block is anything but stock. Displacing 383 inches by way of a 400-cid crankshaft and a .030-inch overbore, the short-block consists of a set of Speed-Pro hypereutectic pistons, rings and bearings, and one of John's own design hydraulic roller camshafts. While he was secretive about the cam timing, John did admit that the cam is very mild, with additional lift over the stock GM grind.

Since cylinder heads are the key to any performance engine, John chose a set of '87 Corvette aluminum heads that received minor port work along with small 1.94/1.60-inch intake and exhaust valves. The key to this engine's power actually lies with the Lingenfelter-modified TPI. Along with enlarged throttle bores, a massaged plenum, and a *mucho*-ported manifold base, John also added a set of his new larger, cast-aluminum runners. While the runners are the same length as stock, they are .125 inch i.d. larger to increase airflow.

On the exhaust side, John chose to retain the stock 1.5-inch Corvette stainless-steel manifolds while eliminating the catalytic converter and bolting on a 2¼-inch Borla stainless-steel dual-exhaust system with Borla mufflers. Before the engine was bolted into the car, John put the engine on his dyno for a quick pull and recorded 368 horsepower at 4500 rpm and an impressive *451 lbs.-ft. of torque* at only 3500 rpm! Those, friends, are big-block numbers!

Since John's plan emphasizes torque rather than horsepower, it's no surprise that he retained the Turbo 700-R4 auto-

Dragstrip-testing the Corvette at Muncie Dragway resulted in a best time of 12.53 at 111 mph. The 'Vette ran best when dumped into overdrive at about the 1000-foot mark! That's what torque will do for you.

matic overdrive transmission along with a 3.55 rear gear. But since the transmission's .70:1 overdrive would still leave the car "overgeared" at 2.48:1, John al-

so added a Gear Vendors overdrive unit featuring a .78:1 ratio. In double overdrive, this put the final-drive ratio at a Bonneville-busting 1.93:1!

Before taking the car to the Ohio Transportation Research Center (TRC) for the high-speed runs, John planned on a quick dragstrip test. Friday morning found us at Muncie Dragway, just outside Muncie, Indiana, to test the Cor-

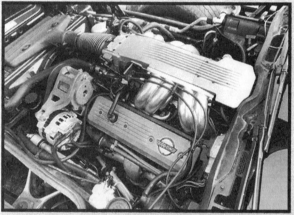

If you were expecting an ultra-high-tech engine with tricks galore, think again. This is simply good old Midwest torque and horsepower from a 383-inch Lingenfelter Mouse motor. Add a pair of his larger TPI runners, a set of ported factory aluminum heads with a very mild hydraulic camshaft, and you have the basics for a 360-horsepower, 450-lbs.-ft. street-masher engine.

As you can see, John has experimented with a number of runner-length configurations to come up with the best compromise between horsepower and torque.

For the top-end run at TRC, John used a set of his larger-diameter, cast TPI runners that were cut back (top) to create shorter runners and a small, secondary plenum area.

MAXIMUM OVERDRIVE

vette's quarter-mile mettle. John decided on a set of Goodyear "S" compound gumball autocross P255/50ZR16 tires for both the dragstrip and high-speed tests, since previous testing had shown that the 383's torque was fully capable of overpowering a set of 8-inch slicks as easily as the street tires.

The weather was hardly ideal since it was both hot and humid, even by 9 a.m. Despite an obvious lack of traction, the Corvette pulled off consistent 12.50s at 111 mph with a 12.53 best effort. Driving the hour back to John's shop did little to underscore the Corvette's abilities. Mild-mannered barely begins to describe how even-tempered the Corvette is in all driving situations. Dropping the car into double overdrive put the cruise rpm at 1600 rpm at 62 mph, and with the Corvette's instant fuel mileage readout, generating 32 to 34 mpg was easy. In fact, on level ground we were able to generate as much as 38-mpg instant readouts at 65 mph! For the total dragstrip trip and test, the 'Vette managed a spectacular 28-mpg figure.

Returning to the shop, John decided to swap to a different set of runners, while also fabricating an air dam underneath the factory aero nosepiece. While I worked on the air dam, "Dyno" Bob and a helper installed the different runners. Everything was running smoothly until 11 p.m., when John discovered a vacuum leak in the intake manifold that required removal of the runners to repair.

What does a Corvette look like at 180 mph? You better look fast, because at that speed, the 'Vette is traveling roughly 264 feet per second! Note the nose-down, tail-up attitude of the car.

"Dyno" Bob returned, and by 1:30 a.m. the car was running fine. But now we were faced with a 1½-hour drive (yes, we *drove* the Corvette—no trailer) to the nearby Holiday Inn.

DAY TWO

The troops were a little on the ragged side at 5 a.m. when we departed the hotel for TRC. We only managed about an hour's sleep because John had scheduled a "dawn launch" at 7 a.m. to take advantage of the cool morning air. By 6:30 we were thrashing to install the air

From inside the passenger compartment, the sensation of speed isn't like accelerating through the quarter-mile, but it's still a thrill! The Corvette was extremely docile at speed, with only a hint of lift in the rear.

dam and remove the exhaust for the test. Since John was attempting 180 mph, he reserved the track exclusively for two one-hour sessions, so the full-court press was on.

While the Midwest was suffering from the worst drought in 50 years, the first session threatened rain, so John put on his helmet, jumped in the Corvette, and jammed out the first pass only to discover that TRC's timing equipment had failed. Twenty minutes later, John tried again and was rewarded with the 176.95-mph pass. With time running out, he convinced the TRC people to relocate the timers at the other end of the 2.5-mile straightaway to benefit from a slight tailwind, but by the time they were ready, we were halted by rain.

Waiting two hours, John tried again with fantastic results. Coming out of the banked turn at 160 mph, the Corvette screamed through the timing trap and the voice on the radio rewarded us with "One Eighty Four Point Three Two Miles Per Hour." Later, John upped this figure to 184.54 to generate a 180.7-mph, two-way average. John's reaction? "It's amazing how going fast can make you feel better."

Afterward, we bolted the exhaust back on, removed the air dam, and drove the Corvette back to John's Decatur, Indiana, shop in air-conditioned comfort, with a short celebration stop at the Dairy Queen. Oh, even with the nine full-power, 180-mph runs and numerous checkout passes, the Corvette still knocked down 18.9 mpg for the round-trip test at TRC. *Maximum Overdrive* indeed! **HR**

	1600	2000	2500	3000	3500	4000	4500	4700	5000	5500
...ected HP	113	146	205	256	300	338	368	364	347	310
...ue (lbs.-ft.)	370	383	430	448	451	443	429	407	364	295

While the horsepower numbers may not be overwhelming, John's attention was placed on building street-usable torque. This is the result of matching the long-runner intake with camshaft, cylinder head, and exhaust components.

The Gear Vendors overdrive is a very compact, self-contained unit that performed flawlessly. It has anvil-like torque capability with a very positive engagement. John engaged the overdrive with a foot-operated switch much like a dimmer switch.

SOURCES

Gear Vendors, Inc.
Dept. HR
365 W. Bradley Ave.
El Cajon, CA 92020
(619) 442-0365

Lingenfelter Racing
Dept. HR
1557 Winchester Rd.
Decatur, IN 46733
(219) 724-2552

The midnight flog on the Corvette delayed our arrival at TRC, but John felt that the addition of the lower air dam was worth at least three to four mph. The only additional aerodynamic work was to remove the outside mirrors.

1 THE BRIEFING

FILLING IN one of those irritating bureaucratic forms at US Customs, Noel Coward replied "Sole purpose of visit" to a question about whether he intended to overthrow the Government of the United States.

My five-day whistle-stop tour of New England and Detroit last April, alas, permitted no time for such revolutionary aspirations. The main purpose of *my* visit was to test the Callaway Twin-Turbo Corvette and to extract as many

features from Motor City as possible.

I had no expectation at the time of driving the ZR-1. Indeed, little was then known about the car, although there had been persistent rumours. When I returned to England I wrote a news story, which was accompanied by an artist's impression of the car, based on my description of it. This appeared under the heading "King Corvette Due Next Year", in our July issue, to accompany the major feature in the magazine on the Callaway car.

Subsequently two UK magazines have published 'exclusive' details on the ZR-1. We didn't call our story 'exclusive' or 'World First' or any such hype, though perhaps we should have done. Also, I didn't publish my driving impressions of the car at the time, because I'd been asked not to

do so.

Two of the basic rules of modern, lager-lout motoring journalism had been ignored: 1 Call it 'EXCLUSIVE' and 2 Never keep a confidence or respect an embargo.

Anyway, I am now in a position to write about driving the ZR-1. This is at least a UK EXCLUSIVE, though perhaps not quite a World First since my friend Mr William 'Don't call me Bill' Jeanes, editor of the American magazine *Car & Driver*, was with me on the same day.

2 THE TRACK TEST

I WAS expecting a briefing on the ZR-1, but no promise had been given of the chance to look at the car at close quarters, still less to drive it. At that time, the ZR-1 was widely known to exist, though better known by its nickname, 'King of the Hill', but no one other than GM personnel had been anywhere near it.

The briefing in the Technical Center, at GM's Milford test track, a few miles from Detroit, confirmed those details which were rumoured and filled in a few others which were news to me. Then, to my great surprise, the invitation was made: "Let's go outside and drive the car." Even then, I thought this would probably consist of sitting in the passenger seat and attempting to give impressions as the car was piloted by a Chevrolet test driv-

er. Some journalists on other magazines have become very skilled at this vicarious driving system, but I can only give anything like an accurate picture of what a car is like if I drive it *myself*.

We drove down from the engineering centre to the test track, and there it was. To my

"The 0-60mph time is predicted to be 4.2sec . . . right up there with the best of the world's crazy toys"

ignorant European eyes, it looked much like a standard Corvette sitting on Countach-sized tyres. "So this is the King of the Hill?" I asked, rather fatuously.

"We don't like that name, but let's go for a drive in the ZR-1," said David McLellan, the Corvette project leader. He pointed out the bodywork changes and moved to the passenger door, so I climbed into the driver's seat. I couldn't quite believe that this was happening, since at that stage no American journalist, let alone a Limey, had sat behind the wheel of the car.

Apart from various items of test equipment, the interior of the test car was much the same as in a standard '88 Corvette, loaded with all the electronic gizmos you could wish for, and a few more besides; some people like it. The only obvious difference was the six-speed gate pattern etched into the top of the gear lever. I turned the key and the 5.7-litre Lotus-developed engine fired up instantly, settling into a recognisable refined V8 tickover, pulsing like a Porsche 928 rather than whining like a Ferrari 328.

In 15 minutes on an unfamiliar test track, it is impossible to reach definitive opinions about the dynamic behaviour of a new car, especially one with all the technical sophistication which has been squeezed into the ZR-1. Milford's high-speed circuit is quite a challenge, not simply a two-mile, flat-out bowl like Britain's Millbrook (recently 'sold' to Lotus by parent company GM), but consisting instead of long straights connected by banked curves of differing ra-

ZF six-speed is positive, slick. Milford test track speed limit 70mph – ZR-1 felt stable at 140 with much more to come.

dius and curvature.

It's awesome if you look too carefully at them on the approach: you are in fourth gear at 130mph on the comfortably wide five-lane straight, and the big 'Vette is still gaining speed, with almost 1,000rpm in hand before the need to change into fifth. Ahead of you the ribbon of concrete folds to the right, and it feels as if you are shaping up to fly a Hercules under Potter Higham Bridge. Best not to look up really. . .

It should be pointed out that I was let loose in something that was clearly a hard-used development hack, and not entirely representative of what may be expected of final production models. Also, at that stage, final specification had not been decided, even in important respects such as the exact power output.

However, first impressions are always interesting, particularly in this case, in a week during which I covered many miles both in a standard 'Vette and in manual and automatic versions of the Callaway Twin-Turbo car (tested in *Fast Lane*, July 1988).

The ZR-1 I drove had a very smooth engine, surprisingly quiet at speed, and with no obvious evidence of unpleasant temperament. The specification suggests that it will propel a ton and a half plus of Corvette very rapidly indeed, and it does not disappoint.

In my short spell behind the wheel it was not possible to judge the potential maximum speed. Initial suggestions of 200mph have been cooled off and look very unlikely in the absence of modifications by Reeves Callaway and his team. The main problem in standard form, apparently, is that the exhaust system is cramped by having to fit within the standard Corvette frame; hence the target output of 400bhp is missed. The car should be good for the 180mph now claimed by the factory, which is enough for anyone whose ego doesn't need an assisted shower. The 0-60mph time is predicted to be 4.2sec, which is half a second better than the current Callaway car can manage, and right up there with the best of the world's crazy toys.

The *basso profundo* growl is delivered in a very relaxed way, even though the engine revs freely to 7,200rpm – and you do have to watch the rev

counter. That makes quite a change from the old small-block Chevy pushrod engine, which signals the need for upward changes by gradually running out of breath. Also particularly good is the throttle action, a crucial factor in the perceived smoothness of any engine. It is clear that *engineers* have been at work here.

As for the gearbox, the quality of the change is a vast improvement over the four-speed-plus-overdrive by Doug Nash used in recent 'Vettes. The ZF gives one of the most positive changes in any current

"Maximum speed will be achieved in fifth rather than top, which is *theoretically* geared to pull 306mph!"

supercar, with a throw that's not too long and feel that isn't too heavy. It simply snicks through from one ratio to the next, more or less as quickly as hand and clutch-foot can move.

Nobody really *needs* six speeds in a road car, especially one that packs under its bonnet something like 380bhp at 6,000rpm and 370lb ft at 4,000rpm (all this being estimated, even at this relatively late stage). But it gets GM off the hook as far as gas guzzler taxes are concerned, and must be an impressive sales tool, especially when applied to the more gullible type of customer. "Lamborghini Countach?

Ferrari F40? You're talking about outdated technology there, I'm afraid, Sir. They only have five gears, you know. . ."

Having six speeds certainly allows relaxed cruising, and you can't get much more relaxed than 42.5mph for every 1,000rpm in sixth: that translates to just over 3,500rpm at 150mph, and it is no surprise that the maximum speed will be achieved in fifth rather than top, which is *theoretically* geared to pull 306mph!

And yes, if you really want to make life difficult for yourself, you can use less than a third of the throttle opening between 12 and 18mph, and find the gear lever slots obstinately into fourth when you try to select second. It's such a minor irritation that it isn't worth the trouble of disconnecting the electronics which govern it; but it does illustrate the absurd lengths to which manufacturers must go in order to satisfy legislation.

It is this government-induced misuse of the time and talents of engineers which enables GM to avoid paying a penalty of five hundred dollars for each car sold, because the ZR-1 set up in this way achieves the required fuel economy (22.5mpg) in the official 'highway' test. Meanwhile, back in the real world. . .

A more intelligent idea is the "Valet key". This means that anyone trusting enough to allow his 17-year-old son out in this machine can at least reduce the severity of the subse-

quent accident by turning a key in a lock in the console. This restricts the power output to 200bhp, by starving half of the 16 inlet ports of fuel, thus effectively running the engine on one intake valve and two exhausts although the other intake valve is actuated, its port is blocked.

No doubt you will forgive me for not investigating this clever device in practice: when you know you've only a few minutes in which to play, you don't want to have only half

the fun. Dave McLellan clearly decided I was over 17.

After we'd completed half a dozen laps, McLellan said apologetically, "I guess I should tell you that there's a speed limit on this track . . ." A test track with a speed limit! Apparently, they don't like people to exceed 70mph, and we'd been travelling at up to 140 or so.

I find it hard to reach definite conclusions about the FX3 Delco-Bilstein three-way suspension system. For one thing, although the test track is bumpy in places, it doesn't reproduce what you can expect to find on public roads. I really couldn't tell you how it would cope with the craters in Man-

Lotus developed and will build cylinder heads for five-litre engine. Suspension and engine highly modified from standard but interior almost unchanged.

hattan, or indeed Birmingham. For another, the left front damper was clearly beyond its operational usefulness, pitching the car into a pronounced corkscrew action from about 130mph. "I'm afraid this car had a pretty tough time last week," McLellan explained.

With the firmest damper setting, though, high-speed stability, apart from that, seemed good. Towards the exit of Milford's most steeply banked curve, a tight righthander which we were exiting at some 120mph or so (and it certainly feels quite tight at that speed), there is a severe dip – put there to examine handling over extreme bumps. That's what GM says it's there for, anyway; it could be simple, old-fashioned subsidence. The car checked quite firmly, and it would be surprising if it did not, but it wasn't thrown violently off line. If it can do that with a loaded corner when not functioning properly, then a fully-fit version promises to be really good.

But I am wary of making any judgements until I have driven the car on a variety of surfaces, preferably in the UK: there have been too many cases of cars which have felt comfortable and well-controlled on their home ground which have subsequently turned out to be less than impressive on Britain's crowned, pot-holed, bumpy byways.

As you'd expect, the big tyres give phenomenal grip and traction, at least on a dry surface, but it isn't at the expense of feel and progression. There isn't a lot wrong with the current Corvette chassis, anyway, now that spring and damper rates have been adjusted so that the car gives not only high g-numbers on a skidpad but also copes well with normal roads, no longer shaking your fillings out over bumpy approaches to bends. The ZR-1 is taken a stage further, with basically similar dynamic response but everything beefed up to cope with the extra grunt.

The standard ZR-1 will not be the world's fastest production car. It promises, however, to be not only the finest Corvette ever built but one of the world's best sports cars, and its classic combination of high-

powered, front-mounted engine and rear-wheel drive, developed with integrity by an outstanding team of engineers, should give the Corvette, Chevrolet and, indirectly, the American car industry in general, a far shinier image in the rest of the world.

It is a pity that there is little prospect of a right-hand drive version, because (as in the standard Corvette) the engine is asymmetrically located.

3 THE TECHNICAL BACKGROUND

THE ZR-1 is not an entirely new design: the piece of paper was not blank and the computer screen already had many of the parameters programmed. However, it constitutes a dramatic evolutionary leap from the basic Corvette, with its virtually all-new engine, new gearbox, and radically revised suspension system. Here are a few basic details.

BODY/CHASSIS

Steel chassis frame integrated with glass-reinforced plastic body. Basically similar to dimensions of standard Corvette body, with identical length, wheelbase, height and even front and rear track but an extra 2in in width.

ENGINE

Developed in association with Chevrolet by Lotus, who will also build the cylinder heads, the LT5 all-aluminium 4,727cc V8 will be built by Mercury Marine (another GM subsidiary) in Oklahoma. It has a narrower bore and longer stroke (99 × 93mm) than the old L98 iron-block Chevrolet engine.

It has four valves per cylinder, a compression ratio of 11.3:1, and GM electronic multi-point injection (one injector for each of 16 intake ports). There are three stages of induction:

1 At idle (only 400rpm) and at low speeds, a narrow valve permits economical running.

2 200bhp setting (limited by power switch in console): eight inlet ports in operation.

3 Hold on to your hats the second set of ports opens up, feeding valves which are activated by cam lobes with a higher duration profile (that is, the valve is held open for longer) than the 'primary' intake lobes. Thus the first set of ports and valves is tuned for low and mid-range torque, while the second set provides the peak power.

Maximum power (estimated) 380bhp/ 6,000rpm

Maximum torque (estimated) 370lb ft/ 4,000rpm

Fitted with full anti-pollution system including three-way catalytic exhaust converter.

TRANSMISSION

Rear-wheel drive, ZF six-speed manual, with limited-slip differential.
Final drive ratio 3.54:1
Internal ratio, mph/1,000rpm, speeds in gears:

First 2.68:1/7.8	56mph/7,200rpm
Second 1.80:1/11.6	83mph/7,200rpm
Third 1.31:1/15.9	114mph/7,200rpm
Fourth 1.00:1/20.8	150mph/7,200rpm
Fifth 0.75:1/27.8	180mph/6,475rpm
Sixth 0.49:1/42.5	151mph/3,550rpm

SUSPENSION/BRAKES/TYRES

Standard Corvette layout, with transverse composite leaf springs and anti-roll bars at each end, location at the front by unequal length double wishbones and at the rear by upper and lower trailing arms, lateral arms and tie rods.

Full suspension specification is not yet decided, but will either be the "Z51" package, with stiff springs and dampers and thick anti-roll bar, or the new Delco Bilstein FX3 Selective Ride Control System.

In this the driver can switch between three damping programmes: Soft, Touring, Sport. A computer controls a rotary valve in each damper by means of small electric motors, and automatically selects one of six settings in each programme according to vehicle speed.

The Z51 braking system, proven on the race-track, is more than adequate for the ZR1, with its massive ventilated discs front and rear, and twin front calipers.

Steering is by assisted rack and pinion, and the Goodyear Eagle tyres are 275/40 ZR 17 on 9.5J front rims and 315/35 ZR 17 on rear 11in rims.

CHEVROLET CORVETTE ZR-1

World-class performance to counter the Countach and tackle the Testarossa

PHOTOS BY JOHN LAMM

THEY GET NO respect, those American-made sports cars. Especially in Europe where performance, handling and exclusivity—not catchy ad slogans—determine the true measure of a car's worth. Sure, the Swiss buy Detroit-built sedans and wagons but one suspects it's an affectation—like wearing denims with your Giorgio Armani jacket. Truth is, most European automotive enthusiasts have little regard for almost any automobile America has produced in recent memory.

Designed by Lotus, built by Mercury Marine and installed in the Corvette ZR-1, the dohc 5.7-liter LT5 engine has a two-phase induction system that helps it to produce 380 bhp yet remain docile at parking-lot speeds.

But with the introduction of the Corvette ZR-1—at the 1989 Geneva auto show, of all places—that attitude is about to change.

You may know the ZR-1 as the King of the Hill, which is what this Super Vette was commonly called when the program was barely more than a rumor. For reasons known only to GM brass, that name is now taboo. Our guess is that Chevy, who's seeking international recognition, found the name too domestic, not to mention too long for a car badge—and untranslatable (*Le roi de la montagne? Non. Der König am Hügel? Nein*). Better to keep it simple, short and sweet. And alphanumeric so as to capitalize on its similarity to other European exotics such as the BMW M1 and Ferrari F40.

Exotic? Dave McLellan, Corvette chief engineer since 1975, prefers you not call it that. As McLellan sees it, exotics are outrageously styled, astronomically expensive, highly temperamental, limited-production automobiles that are often racers masquerading as road cars.

Sure they're fast (180 mph is median speed for most Bahnburners), but if you were going cross-continent, you would take the Merc or the Bimmer. Until now. You see, the ZR-1, one of the fastest sports cars in the world, is also blessed with superior handling and braking. Yet it is the most civilized and technologically advanced and the least expensive super-car in production because it is still a Corvette.

The ZR-1 looks like a Corvette. There's that unmistakable shape but with a notable difference: The bodywork widens beginning at the leading edge of the doors and culminates in a tail that is 3 in. broader than the normal Vette's—to accommodate the hefty P315/35ZR-17 Goodyear Eagle Gatorbacks made specifically for this car. The soft, polyurethane end cap is different too, convex rather than concave with square versus round taillights and a small red ZR-1 badge that graces the lower right corner. Chevy 3 studio chief John Cafaro describes the Vette's physique as "muscular," and this is especially evident in the ZR-1, which shares the same front end (front wheels and tires too) with the conventional Corvette, the so-called L98. Another notable difference between the L98 and ZR-1 is weight. Heftier engine, bodywork, tires, etc. make the Super Vette some 200 lb. heavier than an L98 coupe.

As a Corvette, the ZR-1 also shares the Bosch ABS II anti-lock braking, hybridized Z51 suspension and FX3 Selective Ride Control packages with the L98. Ditto the UJ6 Low-Tire-Pressure Warning System, which along with the above is standard on the Chevy flagship. Although the Bosch ABS and the suspension need no explaining (it's basically the Z51 setup with softer springs and anti-roll bars) and the UJ6 is self-explanatory (a light on the center console tells you if a tire is going flat), FX3 does call for a brief description.

Basically, this Bilstein-engineered system, which borrows from Porsche 959 and Lotus Formula 1 technology, uses a gas-over-oil shock absorber whose hollow center shaft is fitted with an adjustable orifice that allows varying amounts of shock oil to be bled off from around the piston. This provides six levels of damping in each of the three modes, Touring, Sport and Performance, for a total of 14 steps (not 18, because some overlap). Settings range from very soft to full hard in incremental steps that are governed by vehicle speed. Lest you wonder how the system works, let's just say that it's done with servomotors (actuators mounted atop each shock and used to turn the shaft that regulates the oil bypass) and a microprocessor (to sense road condition and speed and to send appropriate information to the servos). True, other high-volume manufacturers have offered cockpit-adjustable shocks, but this is the first use in hyper-performance territory. More about this later when we discuss driving the ZR-1.

Unique to the ZR-1 (and for most of us, its *raison d'être*), the LT5 engine is a lovely example of double-overhead-cam, 4-valve-per-cylinder technology. Developed jointly with Lotus and built by Mercury Marine (the boat motor people), this 5.7-liter aluminum, 32-valve V-8 has the same 4.40-in. bore center spacing (for standardization purposes) as the venerable Chevy small block. To maintain this distance, the bore has been reduced from 4.00 to 3.90 in., while the stroke has been increased from 3.48 to 3.66 in. Aluminum cylinder liners that are lighter than steel are Nikasil-coated, and the externally ribbed block has a cast aluminum oil sump and lower crankcase assembly whose integral 4- and 6-bolt cast-iron main bearing caps secure the forged steel crankshaft. Up top, the LT5's four camshafts are driven by

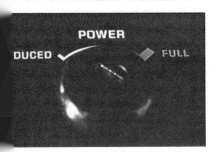

The same, only better: Nestle into that familiar interior, turn the power switch to the FULL position, and take total advantage of the LT5's torque with the 6-speed gearbox.

ZR-1 spotters can look for subtle clues: the convex tail cap, taillights more square than round, and rectangular exhaust tips. More obvious is the incredible way it squirts forward when the accelerator is depressed.

a roller chain (Gilmer belts were considered, but discarded because they would have made the engine too wide to be bottom-loaded into the Corvette chassis on the Bowling Green assembly line) and actuate hydraulic lifters that eliminate valve lash adjustment. The 4-valve combustion chambers feature centrally located sparkplugs (for reduced flame travel) and are designed to act in concert with dished aluminum pistons with an 11.0:1 compression ratio. To ensure that all of this very elaborate (and expensive) machinery doesn't self-destruct for lack of proper lubrication, the engine oiling system holds 12 quarts, seven more than the pushrod V-8.

Nothing unusual so far, you say. Any engine worth its salt has all this. Too right. But no other engine in the world has the LT5's two-phase induction system that makes the Chevy 32-valver two powerplants in one: a tractable, fuel-efficient, around-town workhorse; and a gut-wrenching, full-on track star that hammers out 380 bhp. With its 16 tuned-length intake runners, the visually distinctive manifold uses a 3-valve throttle body with a small primary for responsive low-speed operation and two large secondaries for full-power usage. During normal use only, the primary intake ports and fuel injectors are operative. Mash on the gas and let the revs climb above 3500 rpm or to half-throttle, and the secondary ports and injectors come into play. Acting under orders from the Electronic Control Module, the secondaries feed

the fuel-air mixture to the larger of the two intake valves whose camshaft lobes have more radical timing for maximum power. In addition to making the LT5 the most versatile engine in the world, the two-stage induction system enables the Vette owner to regulate engine operation. A power switch on the console (the so-called valet-parking key) disables the secondary throttles and their injectors, leaving the engine operating at half power—to discourage unauthorized drivers from using the LT5's full potential.

The ZR-1's V-8 uses direct-fire ignition: Four coils ignite two sparkplugs simultaneously, upon receiving their cue from a crankshaft sensor acting in concert with the ECM. Because the sensor reads the position of machined notches on the crank, correct ignition timing is ensured. Spark advance and retardation are electronically controlled by the ECM, which gets an additional bit of information from a knock sensor. Whether idling or at speed, the 32-valver runs no hotter (and generally cooler) than the L98, thanks to its distinctive cooling system with 15-percent larger radiator and relocated thermostat (it's on the inlet side of the engine).

To help deliver the LT5's output to the rear wheels, Chevy has given the ZR-1 and the normal Corvette a unique 6-speed transmission, which uses CAGS (Computer Aided Gear Selection) that automatically short-shifts from 1st to 4th under light throttle. This beefy, ZF-designed gearbox (code-named ML9) replaces the Doug Nash 4+3 manual overdrive tranny used from 1984 through 1988 and is capable of handling at least 425 lb.-ft. of torque, much more than the LT5's respectable 370 lb.-ft. When used with the 32-valver, the 6-speed drives the rear wheels through a 3.54:1 ring and pinion that gives a slightly lower final drive ratio than the L98's 3.33:1.

Of course, the expected Corvette niceties abound (except for the see-through, hard-coated acrylic roof panel, the ZR-1 is what the trade calls "fully optioned out"). This means that, in addition to everything mentioned above, leather-covered sport seats and that great-sounding Delco/Bose system are standard. Paint schemes are standard Corvette and include seven hues, but not the yellow seen on the Geneva show car. Interestingly, there is no climate control, just plain old air conditioning and heating, because at this time the fully automatic system won't clear the right cylinder head.

Considering the car's limited availability (Chevy plans to build only 4000 per year beginning this summer), most early ZR-1s will probably become collector cars, bought at inflated prices and traded at even higher ones. A pity, because if ever there was a car that begged to be driven, and driven hard, this is it. Unlike

CORVETTE ZR-1

PRICE

List price, FOB Detroit **$50,000**
Price as tested **$50,000**
    Price as tested includes std equip. (air cond, leather seats, AM/FM stereo/cassette, anti-theft system, elect. window lifts, removable roof panel, central locking, low tire press. warning, elect. adj mirrors, cruise control).

0–60 mph .... 4.9 sec
0–¼ mi .... 13.4 sec
Top speed .... 172 mph
Skidpad 0.94g
Slalom .... 65.7 mph
Brake rating .... excellent

MANUFACTURER

Chevrolet Motor Division, General Motors Corp,
30007 Van Dyke Ave, Warren, Mich. 48090

PHOTO BY DAVID FRANKLIN

DRAWING BY BILL DOBSON

Curb weight: **est 3530 lb**
Test weight: **est 3680 lb**
Length: **177.4 in.**
Width: **74.0 in.**
Seat width: **2 x 18.5 in.**
Seating capacity: **2**

Height: **46.7 in.**

Track, f/r: **59.6 in./61.9 in.**
Trunk space: **11.6 cu ft**

12 deg
35.5 in.
Fuel capacity: **20.0 gal.**

42.5 in.
5.5 in.

Ground clearance: **4.7 in.**

Wheelbase: **96.2 in.**
Weight dist (with driver), f/r, %: **est 52/48**

ENGINE

Type .... alloy block & head, **V-8**
Valvetrain .... dohc, 4-valve/cyl
Displacement .... 350 cu in./5727 cc
Bore x stroke ....3.90 x 3.66 in./
    99.0 x 93.0 mm
Compression ratio 11.0:1
Horsepower
    (SAE net).. **380 bhp @ 6200 rpm**
Bhp/liter 66.4
Torque ...... **370 lb-ft @ 4500 rpm**
Maximum engine speed .... 7000 rpm
Fuel injection ... Rochester elect. port
Fuel .... prem unleaded, 91 pump oct

CHASSIS & BODY

Layout .... **front engine/rear drive**
Body/frame .... fiberglass body on
    skeletal steel chassis
Brakes
    Front .... **12.9-in. vented discs**
    Rear ...... **11.9-in. vented discs**
    Assist type .... vacuum, ABS
    Total swept area .... 407 sq in.
    Swept area/ton .... 221 sq in.
Wheels .... cast alloy; **17 x 9½ f,
    17 x 11 r**
Tires .... Goodyear Eagle ZR;
    275/40ZR-17 f, 315/35ZR-17 r
Steering ... **rack & pinion**, pwr assist
    Overall ratio 15.0:1
    Turns, lock to lock 2.2
    Turning circle .... 40.0 ft
Suspension, f/r ..... **upper & lower
A-arms,** transverse leaf spring,
tube shocks, anti-roll bar/**multilink**
(upper & lower trailing arms, lateral
arms, tie rods, halfshafts), transverse fiberglass leaf spring, tube
shocks, anti-roll bar

DRIVETRAIN

Transmission .... **6-sp manual**

Gear	Ratio	Overall ratio	(Rpm) Mph
1st	2.68:1	9.49:1	55
2nd	1.80:1	6.37:1	82
3rd	1.31:1	4.64:1	112
4th	1.00:1	3.54:1	147
5th	0.75:1	2.66:1	(6140) 172
6th	0.50:1	1.77:1	(4050) 170

Final drive ratio 3.54:1
Engine rpm @ 60 mph in 6th 1430

INTERIOR NOISE

Idle in neutral .... 53 dBA
Maximum in 1st gear .... 82 dBA
Constant 50 mph .... 73 dBA
    70 mph .... 74 dBA

INSTRUMENTATION

200-mph speedometer, 8000-rpm
tach, oil press., coolant temp, oil
temp, volts, fuel level

FUEL ECONOMY

Normal driving .... est 19.0 mpg
EPA city/highway ..... est 17/26 mpg
Cruise range .... est 360 miles
Fuel capacity .... 20.0 gal.

MAINTENANCE

Oil/filter change ... 7500 mi/7500 mi
Tuneup .... 30,000 mi
Basic warranty .... 36 mo/36,000 mi

ACCELERATION

Time to speed	Seconds
0–30 mph	1.9
0–40 mph	2.8
0–50 mph	3.6
0–60 mph	4.9
0–70 mph	6.0
0–80 mph	7.8
0–90 mph	9.5
0–100 mph	11.5

Time to distance
0–100 ft 2.9
0–500 ft 7.3
0–1320 ft (¼ mi): 13.4 @ 108.5 mph

BRAKING

Minimum stopping distance
    From 60 mph .... 132 ft
    From 80 mph .... 233 ft
Control .... excellent
Pedal effort for 0.5g stop .... 21 lb
Fade, effort after six 0.5g stops from
    60 mph .... 24 lb
Brake feel .... very good
Overall brake rating .... excellent

HANDLING

Lateral accel (200-ft skidpad) .. 0.94g
    Balance .... mild understeer
Speed thru 700-ft slalom .. 65.7 mph
    Balance .... neutral
Lateral seat support .... excellent

Subjective ratings consist of excellent, very good, good, average, poor.

Test Notes . . .

■ The LT5 engine is a marvel: From 1000 rpm, it pulls unfettered; pressing 7000 rpm, there's little tapering in power. Indeed, its tractability rivals that of the best of the 12-cylinders; and its sound, a vintage racing V-8.

■ Considered together, its record 0.94g lateral grip and second-highest slalom speed we've ever achieved are persuasive arguments that the ZR-1 is the most capable handling car in the world.

■ Weighing 200 lb more than a stock Corvette and rolling on wider tires covered by expanded rear bodywork, the ZR-1 feels more substantial. But what it may lose in nimbleness, it more than regains in sheer power and speed.

some exotics that fuss in traffic and fume in hot weather, the LT5 powerplant runs like any good Detroit V-8 should: effortlessly, reliably. In city driving (or while following that ubiquitous diesel truck along a hilly European two-lane), this muscular V-8, which develops 300 lb.-ft. of torque at 1500 rpm, burbles along happily at practically idle speed. So there's no need to do a lot of shifting—or to let your blood pressure soar because you're playing follow-the-leader. Don't worry, be happy, enjoy the air-conditioned stereo-filled environment of your ZR-1 and wait until it's safe to . . . PASS!

Let the record show that after easing off the line at about 1500 rpm to avoid wheelspin, the ZR-1 goes from 0 to 60 in 4.9 seconds and gets to the quarter-mile marker in 13.4 sec. Speed-shifted, Corvette engineer Jim Ingles style, it's a few tenths quicker. When it's time to stop, this 3680-lb. sports car comes to a halt in 132 ft. from 60 mph and 233 ft. from 80 mph. Impressive? You bet! Also, better than the top three exotic cars (Ferrari Testarossa, Lamborghini Countach, Porsche Turbo).

In real-world terms, this level of performance means that, depending on the amount of room you have to do so, you can either ease into the throttle, activate those giant secondaries and sort of swoop past. Or you can downshift a gear or two (because of the 32-valver's 7000-rpm redline, there's plenty more revs than in the normal V-8) and blow by that slowpoke *con brio!* And don't fret about ducking back into your proper lane. Those giant, vented disc brakes and Bosch ABS will stop you quickly and safely, even if it's wet or if the road surface is gravely. Or just in time to slow for that DANGEROUS CURVE.

Not a problem. Lateral acceleration (you can just call it handling) has always been the Vette's forte, but this model sets new standards. Ladies and gentlemen, the new king of the skidpad, the ZR-1. Thanks to its suspension, Selective Ride Control and those sticky ZR-rated (193-mph) Goodyear Gatorbacks, the ZR-1 toes the (curved) mark at 0.94g, better than any production-built automobile, bar none. There's mild understeer and a feeling of comparative nimbleness brought on by steering that no longer feels overboosted and darty (the ratio has been slowed from 13.1:1 to 15.0:1). Nor is the Super Vette a slouch in the slalom where it slithers through the cones at 65.7 mph. It's the second-fastest speed we've ever recorded, topped only by the Mitsubishi Galant, a car with front drive (which the slalom tends to favor) and with a highly sophisticated reactive suspension of its own.

The ZR-1 is a real confidence-builder for a driver who suddenly discovers that a certain constant radius turn, isn't. At times like this it keeps all four feet (or tires) planted firmly on the pavement and maintains its composure—with a deft flick of the wheel or tap of the throttle, if need be.

Much of the credit for this improvement in vehicle attitude and ride goes to the Corvette's Selective Ride Control package. Unlike the suspensions of yore (standard equipment on the 1989 normal Corvette) that provided either soft ride or good handling, FX3-equipped L98 and ZR-1 Vettes offer both—in varying degrees depending on switch setting.

On bumpy roads such as some of the French goat paths encountered during the ZR-1's European press introduction, the Touring mode works best. This soft setting not only keeps one's fillings intact, but also makes the suspension more compliant (better able to absorb much of the road's roughness) and enables the wheels to stay in contact with the pavement.

On smooth, fast roads or on a test track such as Goodyear's Mireval proving grounds near Narbonne, France, the Sport or Performance modes are best. Here, the flat surface ensures that the ZR-1's Gatorbacks are in constant contact with the pavement, so the function of shock-absorber damping becomes one of chassis tuning. Suffice to say that the middle (Sport) setting is probably best (even Corvette Challenge competitors use it), while the full-hard setting makes the suspension very responsive to steering input, and (ahem) quite stiff.

From the outset, the Corvette group sought to make the ZR-1 one of the fastest production-built cars in the world. And so it is, even if those Countach curmudgeons and testy Testarossers quickly point out that its 172-mph top speed falls a few digits short of the Lambo's flat-out 179 mph and the Ferrari's 185-mph figure. Perhaps, they should bear in mind that the ZR-1 was tested in California's high desert with minimal approach room, while the exotics were tested in Europe at Volkswagen's Ehra-Lessien test track where we think, given miles to unwind, the LT5 could manage high 170s. Consider also that the Ferrari and Lamborghini are specially built automobiles costing almost three times as much as the ZR-1, which is built on the same assembly line as the normal Vette. And costs $50,000, a bargain considering the level of performance and comfort it delivers.

But is it, as Chevy hopes, a world-class car? (The envelope, please!)

Yes. The Corvette ZR-1 acquits itself well amidst some very fast company. Yet it does so with a level of sophistication and comfort beyond what most exotics (but not specialty cars such as the Porsche 959) currently deliver. Throw in availability and serviceability (the GM-CAMS computer diagnostic system, mandatory service equipment for all ZR-1 dealers) and you have a car that offers the best of the old and the new world.

AMBASSADOR OF GOOD WHEELS

Chevy's Corvette ZR-1 goes where only the exotics dare tread

BY JOE RUSZ

JUST A FEW kilometers from Carcassone, the road became narrow and twisty. Then it began to climb, up from relative sea level to a thousand feet or more. Magnificent vistas greeted us at every turn, but only my passenger, Corvette Chief Engineer Dave McLellan, dared enjoy them. I kept my eyes fixed on the road ahead, knowing that between us and those panoramas, just beyond the gravel shoulder and grassy verge, was a drop-off that would test the one aspect of the Corvette that is no better or worse than that of any other car in the world—free fall.

We were motoring along in southwestern France, on a 300-mile-long, great circle route that took us north to Lacaune and St. Affrique to St. Rome-de-Tarn, up the spectacular (and narrow) Gorges du Tarn to Ste. Enimie, through Rodez, then south through Albi and Castres, back to Carcassone, the medieval city that served as home base for the ZR-1 introduction.

Medieval city? South of France? Can this be Chevrolet? Yes. There were those who rather insensitively asked, "Why are we here?" But the answer was obvious: Chevy has worldwide aspirations for its world-class sports car. That's why it wouldn't do to introduce it at Detroit or Chicago and to drive it around Black Lake at the GM Proving Grounds. A world-class car belongs in a world-class environment, and Dave McLellan put it best when (in the course of our drive) he remarked, "You won't find roads like these anywhere else in the world." Well, certainly not in Michigan, Toto.

So here we were in Countach country and Testarossa territory in a car that—except for its German ZF gearbox, Bosch ABS and Bilstein adjustable-ride shock absorbers—is as American as pork rinds. Okay, so it's somewhat European-ized. But truly international? Let's just see.

Imagine a test loop not unlike the one set up by our friends at Corvette group who found out, along with the rest of us, that 300 miles on twisty, swooping French two-lanes is a hard day's drive. Choose your favorite exotic or one of the legendary supercars included here and put yourself behind the wheel. Think of the most arduous conditions—narrow roads with blind turns, loose pavement, nerve-jangling Sunday traffic, heat—then try to envision your physical and mental state when the sun disappears behind the Pyrenees and a hot shower and dinner are still an hour away.

If you take the Countach, the ringing in your ears at the end of the day won't be that trans-atlantic phone call. The Lambo is loud inside and out, although no enthusiast with a soul would dare call it noisy. This is music, even if 92 dBA at full song does tiptoe toward the threshold of pain.

With its extremely wide doorsills and low, body-hugging seats, the Countach is a bit awkward to mount, not unlike the Corvette, which, though a bit higher, is also not the car for the Sansabelt slacks crowd.

Tripping through the Monts de Lacaune, you're shifting a bit more frequently than you would in the ZR-1. That's not because the bull-ish dohc, 48-valve, 5.2-liter doesn't have plenty of power (455 bhp and 368 lb.-ft. of torque aren't exactly anemic), but because even with Bosch KE-Jetronic this raucous V-12 isn't quite as tractable as the fully electronic, port fuel-injected LT5 powerplant—nor as fuel efficient. So you'll be eyeing the fuel gauge and mentally counting your cash (high-test costs $3-plus per gallon in France) as you squirt up hill and down dale.

Braking deeply into that sweeper won't be a problem, unless the road surface gets a bit loose. If that happens, the non-ABS-equipped Lambo might give you a few anxious moments before its beefy tires regain their usual firm grip on the pavement. In your haste to (ahem) gather the car up, you'll be using a fair amount of muscle: The Countach steering, while direct and sensitive, does not have power assist.

For an encore, you might try the Testarossa. It's the most civilized true (spelled, Italian) exotic and, yes, the fastest of the factory-built, readily available supercars (Ruf Porsches and

959s don't count). Surprisingly, the ingress/egress of the TR is on par with the average automobile—flat doorsills flush with the floor and seats that you simply slide into (no Jane Fonda workout gymnastics required here). A comfortable, well-appointed interior, air conditioning, stereo sound system, etc., help explain why some Italian *Ferraristi* scornfully call this the American Ferrari.

Perhaps, but a Ferrari nonetheless. The TR does what you'd expect Modena's finest model to do—go like the wind. Its 4-cam, 48-valve flat-12 specs out very close to the ZR-1 in horsepower and torque, delivering the same 380 bhp and nearly identical 360 lb.-ft. at similar rpm. Yet this 5.0-liter is tractable, thanks to its Bosch KE-Jetronic fuel injection that is a vast improvement over carburetors. Unfortunately, this Bosch system does not have the sophistication of the Corvette fuel-management system, which also addresses such problems as knock. So when in doubt, downshift.

But this brawny flat-12 certainly will hustle you hurriedly down the road. Yet, it will behave itself in the interim. Remember, the TR is an Americanized Ferrari. However, it is still a true exotic, which means no anti-lock braking, no power-assisted steering, no rest for the wicked—or the weary.

To automotive purists, the Porsche 911 Turbo is not a true exotic. But its cost, level of performance and supercar image certainly qualify it for the exotic car hall of fame. And for our imaginary trip.

Getting in is no problem. Nor is getting comfortable in the fully equipped interior. The Porsche is civilized, capable of being driven in any environment—quickly. The time-proven, turbocharged 3.3-liter sohc flat-6 pumps out a respectable 282 bhp and develops 278 lb.-ft. of torque. This is far less than the Countach, Testarossa and Corvette, but more than adequate for a car that is 500 lb. lighter than the rest. With its Bosch K-Jetronic, this air-cooled boxer is certainly tractable and fuel efficient. But it's a turbo, and while it may be fun during straight-line, point-and-squirt driving, it can be a challenge in those twisties that call for precise throttle modulation. This means most turns, because with its rear weight bias, the Turbo doesn't take kindly to trailing throttle.

Like the exotics with which it keeps company, the Turbo Carrera is capable of taking any road the French or any other country can dish out—provided the Porsche is in the hands of an accomplished driver, one who understands its handling and knows that as good as the Turbo's brakes may be, they don't have ABS. To this Jedi master, the Porsche is capable of performing as well as any exotic and with far less effort. But at best, it's not nearly as quick, sure-footed and refined as the ZR-1.